Enhancing the Management of Fund Raising

John A. Dunn, Jr., *Editor*
Tufts University

NEW DIRECTIONS FOR INSTITUTIONAL RESEARCH

PATRICK T. TERENZINI, *Editor-in-Chief*
University of Georgia

MARVIN W. PETERSON, *Associate Editor*
University of Michigan

Number 51, Fall 1986

Paperback sourcebooks in
The Jossey-Bass Higher Education Series

Jossey-Bass Inc., Publishers
San Francisco • London

John A. Dunn, Jr. (ed.).
Enhancing the Management of Fund Raising.
New Directions for Institutional Research, no. 51.
Volume XIII, Number 3.
San Francisco: Jossey-Bass, 1986.

New Directions for Institutional Research
Patrick T. Terenzini, *Editor-in-Chief*
Marvin W. Peterson, *Associate Editor*

Copyright © 1986 by Jossey-Bass Inc., Publishers
and
Jossey-Bass Limited

Copyright under International, Pan American, and Universal Copyright Conventions. All rights reserved. No part of this issue may be reproduced in any form—except for brief quotation (not to exceed 500 words) in a review or professional work—without permission in writing from the publishers.

New Directions for Institutional Research (publication number USPS 098-830) is published quarterly by Jossey-Bass Inc., Publishers, and is sponsored by the Association for Institutional Research. The volume and issue numbers above are included for the convenience of libraries. Second-class postage paid at San Francisco, California, and at additional mailing offices. POSTMASTER: Send address changes to Jossey-Bass Inc., Publishers, 433 California Street, San Francisco, California 94104.

Editorial correspondence should be sent to the Editor-in-Chief, Patrick T. Terenzini, Institute of Higher Education, University of Georgia, Athens, Georgia 30602.

Library of Congress Catalog Card Number 85-81889

International Standard Serial Number ISSN 0271-0579

International Standard Book Number ISBN 1-55542-986-6

Cover art by WILLI BAUM

Manufactured in the United States of America

Ordering Information

The paperback sourcebooks listed below are published quarterly and can be ordered either by subscription or single-copy.

Subscriptions cost $40.00 per year for institutions, agencies, and libraries. Individuals can subscribe at the special rate of $30.00 per year *if payment is by personal check*. (Note that the full rate of $40.00 applies if payment is by institutional check, even if the subscription is designated for an individual.) Standing orders are accepted.

Single copies are available at $9.95 when payment accompanies order, and *all single-copy orders under $25.00 must include payment*. (California, New Jersey, New York, and Washington, D.C., residents please include appropriate sales tax.) For billed orders, cost per copy is $9.95 plus postage and handling. (Prices subject to change without notice.)

Bulk orders (ten or more copies) of any individual sourcebook are available at the following discounted prices: 10-49 copies, $8.95 each; 50-100 copies, $7.96 each; over 100 copies, *inquire*. Sales tax and postage and handling charges apply as for single copy orders.

Please note that these prices are for the academic year 1986-1987 and are subject to change without prior notice. Also, some titles may be out of print and therefore not available for sale.

To ensure correct and prompt delivery, all orders must give either the *name of an individual* or an *official purchase order number*. Please submit your order as follows:

Subscriptions: specify series and year subscription is to begin.
Single Copies: specify sourcebook code (such as, IR1) and first two words of title.

Mail orders for United States and Possessions, Latin America, Canada, Japan, Australia, and New Zealand to:
Jossey-Bass Inc., Publishers
433 California Street
San Francisco, California 94104

Mail orders for all other parts of the world to:
Jossey-Bass Limited
28 Banner Street
London EC1Y 8QE

New Directions for Institutional Research Series
Patrick T. Terenzini *Editor-in-Chief*
Marvin W. Peterson, *Associate Editor*

IR1 *Evaluating Institutions for Accountability,* Howard R. Bowen
IR2 *Assessing Faculty Effort,* James I. Doi
IR3 *Toward Affirmative Action,* Lucy W. Sells

IR4	*Organizing Nontraditional Study,* Samuel Baskin
IR5	*Evaluating Statewide Boards,* Robert O. Berdahl
IR6	*Assuring Academic Progress Without Growth,* Allan M. Cartter
IR7	*Responding to Changing Human Resource Needs,* Raul Heist, Jonathan R. Warren
IR8	*Measuring and Increasing Academic Productivity,* Robert A. Wallhaus
IR9	*Assessing Computer-Based System Models,* Thomas R. Mason
IR10	*Examining Departmental Management,* James Smart, James Montgomery
IR11	*Allocating Resources Among Departments,* Paul L. Dressel, Lou Anna Kimsey Simon
IR12	*Benefiting from Interinstitutional Research,* Marvin W. Peterson
IR13	*Applying Analytic Methods to Planning and Management,* David S. P. Hopkins, Roger G. Scroeder
IR14	*Protecting Individual Rights to Privacy in Higher Education,* Alton L. Taylor
IR15	*Appraising Information Needs of Decision Makers,* Carl R. Adams
IR16	*Increasing the Public Accountability of Higher Education,* John K. Folger
IR17	*Analyzing and Constructing Cost,* Meredith A. Gonyea
IR18	*Employing Part-Time Faculty,* David W. Leslie
IR19	*Using Goals in Research and Planning,* Robert Fenske
IR20	*Evaluting Faculty Performance and Vitality,* Wayne C. Kirschling
IR21	*Developing a Total Marketing Plan,* John A. Lucas
IR22	*Examining New Trends in Administrative Computing,* E. Michael Staman
IR23	*Professional Development for Institutional Research,* Robert G. Cope
IR24	*Planning Rational Retrenchment,* Alfred L. Cooke
IR25	*The Impact of Student Financial Aid on Institutions,* Joe B. Henry
IR26	*The Autonomy of Public Colleges,* Paul L. Dressel
IR27	*Academic Program Evaluation,* Eugene C. Craven
IR28	*Academic Planning for the 1980s,* Richard B. Heydinger
IR29	*Institutional Assessment for Self-Improvement,* Richard I. Miller
IR30	*Coping with Faculty Reduction,* Stephen R. Hample
IR31	*Evaluation of Management and Planning Systems,* Nick L. Poulton
IR32	*Increasing the Use of Program Evaluation,* Jack Lindquist
IR33	*Effective Planned Change Strategies,* G. Melvin Hipps
IR34	*Qualitative Methods for Institutional Research,* Eileen Kuhns, S. V. Martorana
IR35	*Information Technology: Advances and Applications,* Bernard Sheehan
IR36	*Studying Student Attrition,* Ernest T. Pascarella
IR37	*Using Research for Strategic Planning,* Norman P. Uhl
IR38	*The Politics and Pragmatics of Institutional Research,* James W. Firnberg, William F. Lasher
IR39	*Applying Methods and Techniques of Futures Research,* James L. Morrison, William L. Renfro, Wayne I. Boucher
IR40	*College Faculty: Versatile Human Resources in a Period of Constraint,* Roger G. Baldwin, Robert T. Blackburn
IR41	*Determining the Effectiveness of Campus Services,* Robert A. Scott
IR42	*Issues in Pricing Undergraduate Education,* Larry H. Litten
IR43	*Responding to New Realities in Funding,* Larry L. Leslie
IR44	*Using Microcomputers for Planning and Management Support,* William L. Tetlow
IR45	*Impact and Challenges of a Changing Federal Role,* Virginia Ann Hodgkinson

IR46 *Institutional Research in Transition,* Marvin W. Peterson, Mary Corcoran
IR47 *Assessing Educational Outcomes,* Peter T. Ewell
IR48 *The Use of Data in Discrimination Issues Cases,* William Rosenthal, Bernard Yancey
IR49 *Applying Decision Support Systems in Higher Education,* John Rohrbaugh, Anne Taylor McCartt
IR50 *Measuring Faculty Research Performance,* John W. Creswell

The Association for Institutional Research was created in 1966 to benefit, assist, and advance research leading to improved understanding, planning, and operation of institutions of higher education. Publication policy is set by its Publications Board.

PUBLICATIONS BOARD
Stephen R. Hample (Chairperson), Montana State University
Ellen E. Chaffee, North Dakota Board of Higher Education
Cameron L. Fincher, University of Georgia
Mantha Vlahos Mehallis, Broward Community College
John C. Smart, Virginia Polytechnic Institute & State University
Penny A. Wallhaus, Northwestern University

EX-OFFICIO MEMBERS OF THE PUBLICATIONS BOARD
Charles F. Elton, University of Kentucky
John A. Lucas, William Rainey Harper College
Patrick T. Terenzini, University of Georgia
Robert A. Wallhaus, Illinois Board of Higher Education

EDITORIAL ADVISORY BOARD
All members of the Publications Board and:
Frederick E. Balderston, University of California, Berkeley
Roberta D. Brown, Arkansas College
Lyman A. Glenny, University of California, Berkeley (retired)
David S. P. Hopkins, Stanford University
Roger G. Schroeder, University of Minnesota
Robert J. Silverman, Ohio State University
Martin A. Trow, University of California, Berkeley

For information about the Association for Institutional Research, write:

    AIR Executive Office
    314 Stone Building
    Florida State University
    Tallahassee, FL 32306

    (904) 644-4470

Contents

Editor's Notes 1
John A. Dunn, Jr.

Chapter 1. Setting Targets for a Successful Capital Campaign 7
Richard L. Bennett, John C. Hays
Development professionals outline the steps and key concepts in planning and evaluation of fund-raising goals and of the potential to obtain gift support for them.

Chapter 2. Microeconomic Perspectives Applied to Development Planning and Management 17
G. Jeffry Paton
A professor of educational administration shows how economic concepts afford fundamental insights into the relationships between development expenditures and gift revenues.

Chapter 3. Comparative Studies of Fund-Raising Performance 39
John A. Dunn, Jr., Dawn Geronimo Terkla, Audrey Adam
Institutional researchers suggest an approach to comparative and longitudinal studies of fund-raising progress, expenditures, productivity, and related development office activities.

Chapter 4. Measuring and Expanding Sources of Private Funding 55
Bruce A. Loessin, Margaret A. Duronio, Georgina L. Borton
Senior fund raisers identify a variety of nontraditional sources of funds and unconventional approaches to fund raising, and explore ways of measuring an institution's success with them.

Chapter 5. Understanding and Predicting Alumni Giving Behavior 69
Michael S. Connolly, Rene Blanchette
An institutional researcher and a development researcher develop a case study showing how graphics, survey research, and multivariate statistical techniques can help development professionals better understand and predict alumni giving behavior, both on an aggregate and individual basis.

Chapter 6. Bringing It All Together 91
John A. Dunn, Jr.
A taxonomy of the factors in fund-raising planning provides a checklist for areas where the researcher and the development professional can collaborate.

Index 97

Editor's Notes

What characteristics of an activity make it interesting to the institutional research (IR) professional? One might list the following: impact in shaping the institution's present and future programs; susceptibility to statistical analysis, planning, and management; growing importance to the institution; and attention and involvement by the institution's president. Yet there are activities with these characteristics that have failed to attract IR scrutiny: fund raising and development.

This volume is intended to serve two purposes: to introduce IR and planning professionals to development concepts and vocabulary; and to identify areas for study and techniques for analysis in the development world.

There is no doubt about the growing importance of private fund raising. The Council for Financial Aid to Education estimates that private giving to higher education rose two and a half times in the decade between 1974–75 and 1983–84, from $2,160,000,000 to $5,600,000,000. This voluntary support outpaced both inflation and institutional expenditures; private giving grew from 5.55 percent to 6.22 percent of expenditures in that period.

While independent colleges and universities have traditionally depended more heavily than public ones on voluntary support, public institutions have begun aggressively to solicit private gifts. In 1979–80, public institutions received 28 percent of total giving, and placed five institutions or systems among the twenty receiving the greatest support. By 1983–84, public institutions received 32 percent of voluntary support, and earned nine of the twenty-two top spots.

Fund-raising dollars, though usually only fourth or fifth among the sources of revenue for colleges and universities, can have a disproportionate impact in shaping their programs. Presidents and deans aggressively seek gifts for the facilities or endowment or curricular projects critical to the institution's development; they allocate unrestricted gifts the same way. Projects that attract support go forward; those that do not, however deserving, are left in the starting blocks.

I have found sharing drafts with valued colleagues to be indispensable. Special thanks for their imaginative and creative work go to the contributing authors in this volume. In addition, I am indebted to Steven S. Manos, Peter C. McKenzie, Roger Broome, and Nina Mayer at Tufts University for their thoughtful questions and insightful suggestions; and to Marvin W. Peterson and Patrick T. Terenzini, series editors, for their constructive guidance throughout the project.

Competition for these funds is stiffening, as schools cope with declining support from other sources, and try to arm themselves for sharper struggles to attract students and key faculty. No national statistics are available on the resources that colleges and universities expend in pursuit of private giving. It is the editor's belief, however, that these expenditures have been rising even faster than fund-raising proceeds, as schools with traditionally strong programs exert even greater efforts and schools that have never taken fund raising seriously gear up for that pursuit.

Given these changes, it is surprising and counterproductive that institutional research and planning offices have so little contact with their colleges' and universities' development efforts.

Fund raising is often viewed by its practitioners as an art, not a science. They may contend that development is not susceptible to analysis and management in the traditional sense. A complicating factor in some institutions is that development may be set up as a separate corporation, not fully under the control of the senior administration.

This frequent isolation of development can have unfortunate consequences. IR and planning professionals are held at a distance from an essential (often a driving) component in the institution's growth and development. In turn, development officers are deprived of the insights and planning assistance that researchers and planners could bring.

This volume is intended to help build bridges, starting from the IR side of the chasm. It is not a how-to book on fund raising. Instead, it is an introduction to basic concepts in fund-raising planning and a sampler of analytic studies and procedures. We believe these can be important to IR and planning officers as they begin to work with their fund-raising counterparts—and that they may suggest to development professionals some of the ways in which IR can be helpful. We are writing for institutional research and planning personnel, for development officers who see the need for analytic and research support, and for senior managers who deal with IR, planning, and development. Our aim is to stimulate further work in this area, to suggest areas for methodological development, and to help development and IR professionals work together to improve the management of an increasingly important institutional activity.

Chapters One and Two of this volume deal with goal setting: How do you know how much to go after, and what amount is reasonable to spend on the effort?

Since fund raising is new territory to many institutional researchers, Richard L. Bennett and John C. Hays, development professionals at Stanford University, provide a guided tour of the planning that makes for successful campaigns. They deal with such questions as setting and testing the feasibility of fund-raising objectives; measuring gift potentials; projecting the pattern of giving needed; and assessing the other factors necessary for the campaign to achieve its goals. In addition to introducing the reader to the vocabulary and key concepts, they offer useful cautions based on extensive experience.

G. Jeffry Paton, a professor of educational administration at the University of Rochester on temporary assignment as development planner, identifies the economic concepts that underlie current development practices. He analyzes giving in terms of predisposition and capacity, and emphasizes the important distinction between average and marginal returns on development expenses. After reviewing the available studies of fund-raising costs, he identifies the development of a methodology for systematic monitoring of these expenditures as a key task for institutional research.

Chapters Three and Four focus on performance: How do you know how well your institution is doing in comparison with its own history and with its peers? How are you doing in reaching traditional and nontraditional constituencies?

John A. Dunn, Jr., Dawn Geronimo Terkla, and Audrey Adam of the institutional planning office at Tufts University outline methods for studying fund-raising proceeds (cash received), and fund-raising progress (cash and pledges), expenditures, and productivity. While the focus is on interinstitutional comparisons, the same procedures are useful for longitudinal studies of one's own institution. The authors identify a number of other activity and context areas for analysis.

Bruce A. Loessin, Margaret A. Duronio, and Georgina L. Borton, members of the development office at the University of Pittsburgh, identify a number of nontraditional sources of support and approaches to fund raising. They focus on the need for careful planning of development activities, ways of measuring success in reaching the nontraditional as well as the more usual sources of support, and pose challenges for institutional researchers in devising quantification systems and standards for collecting and analyzing data in these areas.

Chapter Five deals with prospects: How can you identify prospects and their potential? Michael S. Connolly and Rene Blanchette, an institutional researcher and a development researcher at Wesleyan University, present a case study showing how institutional research methods can be helpful in understanding giving patterns among alumni groups, and how they may identify specific individuals with greater or lesser potential.

Finally, Chapter Six constitutes a summary of this work in progress. In addition to pointing out current work in the field, the chapter brings together ideas mentioned throughout this volume for activities in which institutional research and development professionals can collaborate.

Before plunging into the substantive content of the volume, a word about the state of the art would be appropriate. With respect to gift reporting, the long-term and continuing efforts of the Council for Financial Aid to Education (CFAE) to provide comprehensive and useful survey results have been enormously helpful. A recent major contribution was made by the Council for Advancement and Support of Education (CASE) and the National Association of College and University Business Officers (NACUBO) in their 1981 publication, *Gift Reporting Standards and Management Reports for Educational Institutions*. Having the accountants and the development officers in agreement was a significant step.

On the expenditure side, things have moved more slowly. In Chapter Two, Paton cites the need for "the identification of straightforward procedures for estimating [and analyzing] expenditures attributable to development programs and activities," and pointed out that the "trade-off between practicality and methodological perfection and comprehensiveness is critical." He and the editor are currently working with fifteen private universities in a study of fund-raising cost effectiveness. The basic approach being followed is that outlined in Chapter Four. However, we believe that a number of similar studies should be carried out in different sorts of organizations and with different methodologies, before an attempt is made to articulate a single methodology that should be followed. In a parallel effort, Dr. Deirdre A. Ling of the University of Massachusetts at Amherst has initiated a data-sharing effort on staffing and expenditures and organization among development officers of seventeen public universities in the northeastern United States.

In February 1986, CASE received substantial grant support from the Lilly Endowment for a three-year joint project with NACUBO and a small number of colleges and universities "to collect, analyze, and distribute information on what it costs to raise money on America's campuses. The goal of the project is to develop a management process using uniform standards and definitions for reporting expenses so that an institution can do the following: (1) document what is spends to raise funds; (2) [compare those expenditures] with the costs in prior years; (3) monitor the effects that public relations and alumni activities have on how much money [the] institution raises; and (4) compare the costs of fund raising with those at similar institutions" (CASE, 1986, pp. 1-2). Richard Edwards at CASE is in charge of the project.

With support from the Exxon Education Foundation, Professor Robert Carbone at the College of Education, University of Maryland at College Park, has undertaken a program of research on fund raising. The project includes an invitational conference held last year, support for master's and doctoral theses that address significant questions related to fund raising and fund raisers, and a three-year study of the career development and professionalization of fund-raising personnel.

The authors would be particularly interested in knowing about any further studies in this area, in order to support and further develop these methodologies.

John A. Dunn, Jr.
Editor

Reference

Council for Advancement and Support of Education, Press Release, March 14, 1986, concerning grant from the Lilly Endowment.

John A. Dunn, Jr., is vice-president for planning in the Institutional Planning Office at Tufts University.

Undertaking a capital campaign requires considerable planning and critical evaluation of both the needs and the potential to obtain gift support for them.

Setting Targets for a Successful Capital Campaign

Richard L. Bennett, John C. Hays

With a number of major fund-raising campaigns underway, a capital campaign may appear to be a relatively easy undertaking. Those who have been involved in a campaign, particularly those who do this as a profession, will unanimously agree that a successful campaign, like the beginning of a new development office or a sudden need to seek funds for a project, requires the same elements of assessment, planning, and execution. There are no secrets for a successful campaign—unless thorough planning and research are secrets held by those who have mounted a successful campaign. In every case, a campaign requires a well-reviewed list of fund-raising objectives, current information about available gift resources, and sources of other revenues (for example, tuition income, tax-exempt bonds or other forms of debt securities, federal and state funds, and income from endowment).

The traditional question has been, "How do we know how much we can raise?" In this chapter we focus on the many aspects of that question. First, we separate setting the objectives from setting a total goal; we talk about separately testing the feasibility of the objectives and the total amount. Then we delve into the area of measuring the gift potential of the specific donor prospects, and the area of actually making the gift projections. Finally, we conclude with some remarks about checking some other vital resources beyond prospective donors.

In summary, goal setting involves asking oneself a set of clearly defined questions about sources of support without limiting oneself to considering fund-raising resources alone. Unless each aspect is carefully planned, it is certain that at some point during the campaign one will be facing an unexpected problem. While careful planning does not eliminate problems, one's role as the director of the development operation for the campaign will be made much easier by having a thoroughly researched and organized plan in place and operating.

Setting Objectives

Although setting objectives and testing feasibility are well-understood principles, they are worth reviewing. The priorities of a charitable institution are complex and include a number of activities from maintenance of the plant, to providing funds for key, emerging programs, to providing the endowment base so vital to an organization's longevity. Most of these priorities would appear, at first glance, to be legitimate fund-raising objectives, and, indeed, priorities for a development operation. While this is true, the specific area of support may or may not lend itself to fund raising. For example, most organizations possess an infrastructure that requires maintenance. Oftentimes, as in the case of universities, this would include such items as the road, telephone, electrical, and plumbing systems. Apart from their inclusion in specific buildings, much of the physical plant and the cost of maintaining the plant are not particularly attractive gift opportunities. Thus, not all institutional priorities can be translated into fund-raising priorities.

The question then becomes: Who decides the extent of fund raising's participation in determining institutional priorities? The answer is quite simple. It is *not* the chief development officers. Rather, it is a group of individuals that *includes* the chief development officer. In a university it would include the president, the provost, the board of trustees, and the deans of the various schools. In a museum it would include the director, the curators of the different departments, and the chief financial officer. In addition, as many individuals as can practically participate in this discussion should be invited to do so, if only to provide them an opportunity to express an opinion or define a need. For example, in development operations the faculty will plan an important role in communicating the university's needs.

In establishing the list of campaign objectives, the development officer plays a leading role, in that he or she will be the individual most responsible for ensuring that other leaders in the institution generate a list of objectives that properly reflects the needs of the institution *and* that can be sold to an outside audience.

Therefore, the first question a chief development officer might ask himself or herself upon viewing the list of objectives is: How exciting are they? A new building or wing for a museum or an endowment for a department that has an international reputation is more likely to be supported than an objective—of which there are many—that would consume substantial internal resources without yielding a reasonable fund-raising result.

Another pitfall is a set of objectives based on political compromises. That is, the chief development officer, through the president and other principal officers of the organization, must avoid adding objectives to a campaign solely to please an advocacy group within the organization. Campaigns are seldom a success if internal politics force their way onto the agenda.

A major question when considering the objectives is controlling donor access. Once objectives have been established, individuals who have supported the institution in the past are often considered as the most probable prospects for more than one objective. The chief development officer, in conjunction with his or her colleagues, must establish a discipline of control over allocation of and access to prospects. Thus, the chief development officer must ask himself or herself: How disciplined is our academic priority-setting process and how careful are we at allocating prospects and coordinating their solicitations among the various interests within the organization?

While it is easy to engage internal advocates who are interested, this priority-setting process is perhaps the first important time to engage the members of the board of trustees. Not only will they be responsible for making the final judgment about these objectives but, if properly constituted, the board represents the institution's best initial prospects. Therefore, their early engagement not only fulfills an official responsibility but is also the first step in the cultivation and solicitation process.

Feasibility

A discussion of setting objectives for a major campaign cannot be conducted without a careful analysis of the objectives set against the prevailing market, donor interest, and the economy. The development office should undertake this analysis as soon as a set of preliminary objectives is sufficiently formed. The development office will conduct this feasibility test on two levels: macro and micro.

Testing the macro feasibility of such an undertaking is to develop an understanding of how much a particular institution could raise during a specific period, whereas the micro feasibility would be testing each specific objective against known donor interests.

Having the two levels of feasibility analysis, that is, the total that we might raise and the amounts we might raise for each objective, allows us to balance each against the other so that in the end we will have a campaign target that is the sum of reasonable objectives, not the forced fit of objectives to a possible grand total.

Experienced development staff can give a good first approximation in testing both micro and macro feasibility. However, many a campaign has run into difficulty and not been able to accomplish some or a number of its objectives because there has not been a sufficiently careful analysis of the objectives and the institution's fund-raising potential.

In testing macro feasibility the development office should carefully assess its history of giving, including the areas that have received the greatest support, to establish a thorough and *current* understanding of the nature of the institution's gift base.

Specifically, we have used a ten-year history of (1) total giving, (2) total giving to the areas that the campaign will include, (3) giving to the three broad categories of endowment, expendable, and buildings, and (4) giving to such specifics as professorships, dormitories, scholarships, or science buildings. The means to collect this information have been improved over the last decade by the creation and use of computer software that helps keep track of not only who and how much, but also at this juncture in the campaign planning, what objectives donors might support.

To develop an understanding of what might interest and motivate prospects, a survey of major prospects can go a long way toward measuring attitudes and thereby help gain a better understanding of the relative attractiveness of preliminary objectives and themes. Probably such a survey must be buried in an all-alumni survey.

An early, clear understanding of which objectives are likely to be successful enables the organization's officers to discuss these objectives with the institution's friends to ascertain the comparative attractiveness of the emerging objectives. In particular, the institution can better understand whether potential donors consider these needs to be legitimate.

The last test of feasibility is the *nucleus fund*. It also represents the transition from planning to campaigning. Results here predict both the likelihood of the gross amount and the relative success of individual gift objectives. Perhaps the most difficult, error-prone, yet important study that should be undertaken prior to a campaign is this testing of feasibility of specific objectives.

Measuring Gift Potential

Projections are the extension of facts gathered from actual experience coupled with reasonable measures of progress based on a number of factors. The two most important factors are the identification of prospects including an estimate of their capacity, and good records of the institution's past fund-raising history.

As to identification of prospects, it is not enough to say that anyone within a certain geographical area or who has walked through the doors of a particular institution represents a prospect. The danger inherent in this reasoning is that the institution runs the risk of spreading its limited resources across too wide a population. The purpose of measuring gift potential is to draw more specific and clearly understood boundaries around groups of individuals, corporations, or foundations—to pinpoint true prospects and reject unrealistic ones.

For our last campaign we built gift tables for each source (Corporations, Foundations, Bequests, Individuals), but not for each objective. Table 1 shows our gift table target for Individuals and the amounts we actually received. For our next campaign we are going to try to build gift tables like this for each objective.

Where does the fund-raising organization begin? The first question one should ask oneself is: How good is our research and how large an effort are we willing to undertake to develop information about current prospects and donors, and what are our means to identify those who have not yet been identified? It would not be a surprise to anyone to realize that the greatest change in any prospect group, especially organizations with alumni, involves those who have recently accumulated wealth.

Identification and quantification of a prospect group is a dynamic process and research must reflect this. It is not sufficient to stay with the same old list—any unresearched list more than seven years old is outdated and should not be used as a basis for determination of campaign feasibility. (See Chapter Five for a case study on prospect research.)

New constituencies beyond the traditional alumni for an academic institution or membership list for museums or cultural organizations must be explored. These constituencies represent not only corporations and foundations in the area, which in the past two decades have become well known to all charities, but also possible constituencies outside the typical geographic area. Perhaps the most outstanding example of this is the redefinition of what constitutes a prospect population for such charities as

Table 1. Sample Gift Table

Gift Range	Target Donors	Target Amount	Actual Donors	Actual Amount
$10,000,000 and above	2	$ 25.0 million	1	$ 15.0 million
$ 5,000,000 to $10,000,000	3	18.0	1	6.7
$ 1,000,000 to $ 5,000,000	16	19.0	11	18.3
100,000 to $ 1,000,000	165	30.9	145	42.6
Under $100,000		32.1		30.4
		$125.0 million		$113.0 million

the National Wildlife Federation, the Metropolitan Museum in New York, and the San Francisco Cable Car Foundation. In each case, what might have appeared to be limited to a local fund-raising organization or special interest was converted to a national program. While it is reasonable to assume that constituencies distant from the particular activity and its benefits cannot be counted on for annual support, special needs emphasizing the value of that institution to the nation can be quite persuasive in securing capital gifts. Chapter Four expands on these points.

Another element to be measured is the "campaign effect," the amount of gift support that would be received in addition to the current level of giving. Additional questions would include: What would be the form of those contributions and what is the likely pledge rate? It is important to keep in mind that a capital campaign seeks pledges or commitments for gifts in the future rather than a single, present gift. When undertaking a major campaign one should be careful not to commit the proceeds at a rate faster than they are likely to be received. In addition, an institution seeking additional income is likely to receive gifts in unusual forms such as appreciated assets and gifts that reserve life estates.

Making Projections

In making projections, every chart that has ever been shown to a board of trustees or, in fact, to fund raisers themselves, shows a smooth curve with a sudden increase to reflect the "campaign effect." The fact is that if one looks at totals from year to year one is likely to see, particularly with large gifts from individuals, an upward-moving sawtooth. The reason this occurs is that the period required to raise a large gift is most often greater than twelve months. As a result, a solicitation started in one year will not be finished until the following year or so. Therefore, in one year a gift or pledge is recorded that was being worked on in prior years. It is important to anticipate this phenomenon as it will help explain fluctuations during the campaign period and avoid possible confusion or disappointment.

Many development officers wonder what type of projection is most accurate. While there is no specific answer to this question, it is useful to briefly review the basic types of projections. The two basic forms are a percent gain based upon past experience and a straight-line overall projection. It is important to understand that capital campaigns tend to seek gifts in areas not typically received, and thus not reflected in historical results. Therefore, projections made from historical results against newly emerging campaign needs ought to be carefully considered so as not to draw too much from the historical data.

Another question is how optimistic or conservative should these projections be and, further, what distinctions should be made when applying a campaign effect to reflect different types of donors. For example, the same inducements to give will elicit different responses from corporations and foundations and from individuals. Therefore, the projection must be the aggregate of forecasts for each type of donor. The projection should be slightly optimistic: about 7 on a scale from 0 to 10, with 10 being the most optimistic. This factor is really a reflection of the campaign effect and can represent as much as a 10 or 15 percent increment over the period of the campaign.

Another consideration is the rate at which spendable gifts will be received. This can be a surprise to many institutions because often some of the largest gifts will be pledges or gifts that reserve benefit of the income for the life of the donor and other beneficiaries. Further, one should be careful about using the actuarial tables to predict the number of years for which the proceeds would become available for the institution's use. To be conservative and, in many cases, more accurate, an institution should estimate the income beneficiary will continue to receive the benefits for a period of 10 to 15 percent longer than that which is predicted by the tables used to determine the charitable remainder.

The redirection of current donors is not always possible to the extent that internal advocates would like. This can have a powerful effect upon the projections of the money a campaign might raise, because a significant portion of income for a successfully concluded campaign assumes the transfer of interest and thus the gift from areas currently receiving support to those that are not. Then an institution must consider to what degree the development office is capable of redirecting income into the newly emerging objectives, particularly if they represent needs that traditionally have not received substantial support (for example, new buildings or rehabilitating older ones).

More research needs to be done on fund raising for buildings. In 1981, Cambridge Associates developed some information about campaigns with building objectives which indicated that while most or all of the campaigns reached their aggregate goals, their objectives for buildings did not. Although they failed to reach their goals, they were successful in that substantial income was received for buildings. Perhaps the goals were set too high. Often, an institution announces a campaign goal that is about 200 percent of the gift income that it would normally receive during the same period. At the same time, it sets a building goal five to eight times greater than the level of support the institution had been receiving for that purpose.

A test to see if the goal is properly sized is done by making gift tables *for each objective* or group of objectives. Once the tables are completed and aggregated, the development officers can see if a sufficient number of prospective donors exist for each level of giving. This exercise not only helps to confirm the realism of the goal, it identifies cases where a person is considered a prospect for more than one project.

Checking Other Resources

Before announcing a campaign, an institution should carefully review the resources available to achieve the objectives set forth in the campaign. To put it simply, are the staff and budget sufficient to achieve the task?

In a start-up situation, the same broad areas must be questioned, but the specific questions will be slanted differently. For example, instead of measuring the experience of the staff, one should ask about levels of training that will be required.

Development Staff. This is the institution's key to the management of a successful campaign. In analyzing staff, one ought to measure, at least impressionistically, the experience of the staff to determine if there is sufficient distribution of strengths in marketing and planning, management, and field staffing. In looking at the development staff, presidents of institutions should also develop an impression of the energy level of the group and the areas in which additional training or hiring will be necessary.

Volunteers. Questions the chief development officer or the leader of the institution should be asking about volunteers include: How effective have they been in the past and what is their potential to double or triple their level of activity? It is also necessary to have an accurate estimate of the size of the effort required to train volunteers. Finally, one must consider the number of solicitations a volunteer is expected to make at each level, and whether or not the load is reasonable.

President, Provost, Deans. As the solicitations become larger, the president, provost, and other officers of the organization will become more involved in the solicitation of prospects. Their capability of performing effectively in this role and the time they make available for it will be an important element in the size and nature of the campaign. Often upon entering a campaign, development professionals find that the president, provost, and others in the organization are already spending a substantial amount of time with development matters. The question becomes: Have they been performing the type of activity that will be useful in a campaign and conversely, to what extent will they be required to reduce other activities, such as working with lower-level donors, in order to take on the responsibilities related to the campaign?

The development professional will find it necessary to analyze where the leaders of the organization have been spending their time, and if it can be redirected to the primary objectives of a campaign.

Support Services. Before announcing a major campaign, the increased workload on the organization requires a thorough review as does the level of preparedness of the support services. Support services include the record section, gift and pledge accounting, prospect research, publications, stewardship, the alumni association, public events, and computer support. In assessing the preparedness of these groups, one should carefully assess their ability to perform at the level that would be necessary during the campaign. Questions one should ask are: Is this organization prepared to handle x number of publications over the next y years? Are we prepared to provide stewardship for z number of new prospects? How many public events should we have and where should they be held? Is there sufficient staff to support this operation? Are proper computer equipment and software in place to handle the increased volume required for research and coding of gifts as well as retention of special information pertaining to prospect solicitations?

Communications Plan. This plan is the roadmap for publicizing the campaign. The more comprehensive and carefully considered the plan, the more organized the campaign will be in the minds of both the volunteers and those who will be asked to give. No one wants to volunteer for something disorganized or that does not appear to be successful.

A campaign plan, when successful, provides the necessary momentum and organization to keep all those involved in the campaign, both internal and external, moving in the same direction and in unison—but it must be defined and kept alive through an effective program of communications.

Summary

To summarize, the key points made above and in other parts of this volume are based on how well you know your institution, its needs, the reasonableness of those needs, and whether you have made a reasonable assessment of the prospect population and their aggregate potential to contribute.

In entering a campaign, an institution should be certain that it compares itself with comparable institutions. It *is not helpful* to draw comparisons from institutions you would like to emulate when the audience to whom you will commit your staff, volunteers, financial resources, and hopes for success, sees you in a different light. For example, a large, private research university will not find a great deal of guidance if it compares itself with a small, regional college or vice versa. While this is an extreme example, institutions providing the same benefit to society, for example, education, do so in quite different ways and to a wide range of constituencies. Therefore, it is dangerous for one institution to assume that by some additional effort or increase in income they can experience the same results as another institution. It is, however, important to make comparisons. If the institution does compare itself to similar ones, investments in staff and expenditures help the institution to move along a continuum relative to comparable instutitions, and analyses based upon these comparisons are more accurate. Chapter Three details an approach to comparative studies.

Another aspect of a campaign which can seriously affect outcome is that of personalities. Proper planning and process are vital. No matter how eager and forceful the personalities involved, the campaign that follows a premature public announcement made in advance of any research and assessment of feasibility of campaign objectives can have an institution struggling to catch up, thereby wasting valuable resources in order to appear to be organized.

Another must is to set a reasonable campaign target. To understate a target will result in a campaign that reaches its goal so early that prospects and donors begin to doubt the planning ability of the organization, or worse, since the objective has been reached their personal commitment is reduced or eliminated. The other extreme is equally dangerous, both for the campaign and the long-term success of fund raising. An institution should not succumb to the donor or leader who tends to select a number in such a manner that it does not relate to the facts gathered through prospect research and careful analysis.

Finally, it should be understood that a campaign is a time to attempt the unusual—but not the startling. A reasonable goal stated in clear, positive, and hopeful terms is the best means by which an institution can make itself visible among the myriad institutions, all of whom seek money from the same individuals, corporations, and foundations. A campaign will succeed if it reflects thoughtful planning each step of the way.

Reference

Cambridge Associates, Inc. *MIT-Stanford-Ivy League Conference Report: Recent Trends in Physical Plant Giving.* Boston: Cambridge Associates, Inc., Sept. 1981.

Richard L. Bennett and John C. Hays are associate campaign director and director of leadership gifts, respectively, at Stanford University. Stanford is regularly among the top institutions in the country in levels of private support.

Straightforward application of simple economic concepts affords fundamental insights into the nature of relationships between development expenditures and gift revenues.

Microeconomic Perspectives Applied to Development Planning and Management

G. Jeffry Paton

Few issues attract more intense interest or engender livelier debate among development officers than the subject of the appropriate magnitude of investment in development and the optimal deployment of this investment to achieve the best results. What is the appropriate level of expenditure?

This question underscores a difficult task that development officers must confront on a continuing basis: *planning* and justifying the investment of resources in development activities, based on realistic expectations about overall goals and the costs of achieving them.

Under the best of conditions, development managers and academic officers attempt to identify attainable but ambitious giving targets in order to stretch the capacities of development staff and to challenge the benevolence of donor prospects. The planning process is a negotiated trade-off between the magnitude of targets and resource requirements to achieve them; that is, a trade-off between giving goals and development expenditures.

All too frequently, financial jeopardy subverts the development planning process; giving targets are dictated primarily by academic needs rather than by necessarily realistic development aspirations. In this case, the financial urgencies that inspire ambitious development goals typically also constrain investment to reach the goals.

Under normal circumstances, estimating budgetary needs for development is important. In times of financial exigency the estimation is critical. Development goals and budgets must reflect realistic expectations rather than wishful thinking.

My charge, to identify relevant microeconomic perspectives to improve the planning and managing of resource use, requires neither new analytical ideas nor application of concepts and methods unfamiliar to fund raisers. Rather, the effort is one of identifying and explicitly acknowledging the economic concepts reflected in the common perceptions and conventional wisdom guiding current development practices.

This chapter is organized in four main sections and a brief conclusion. The first two sections propose a simple conceptual framework for thinking about relationships between development expenditures and gift revenues. Results of research about these relationships are summarized and discussed in the third section. The fourth section examines some practical applications of the concepts and research results, with special attention to important limitations and qualifications. The concluding section reviews the prospects for continued progress in applying these concepts and methods to improve understanding of development performance. This review suggests several prerequisites for effective research about the development profession.

Simple Relationships Between Expenditures and Giving

A few introductory comments about the examples that follow are appropriate. This description attempts to preserve a convenient consistency in the several tables and figures presented to illustrate the proposed concepts and methods. All of the figures employ the same format and the same variables on the horizontal axis (Expenditures) and vertical axis (Gift Revenues). This consistency simplifies the discussion greatly, and, it is hoped, contributes to the clarity of the descriptions and explanations.

The examples illustrate highly simplified representations of the relationships examined. This useful simplicity, although unrealistic in detail, faithfully represents the most important characteristics of the proposed relationships—the consistent, relatively stable features that underlie the more volatile idiosyncrasies of fund raising and giving.

This discussion employs two simple measures—*"returns* to development expenditures" and *"costs* of giving"—to express the same relationship between expenditures and giving. These expressions are, of course, reciprocals of one another. If the cost of each gift dollar is one-tenth of a dollar (or ten cents), then the return for each dollar of expenditure is ten dollars. The text occasionally switches from one to the other of these reciprocal measures of development performance, depending on the convenience afforded by one or the other in the particular context of the usage.

Estimating returns or costs is difficult. The best methods can only represent the direct relationship between expenditures and gift revenues in a single year or the typical relationship that prevails over a longer time period. The causal relationships between fund-raising efforts and giving are neither direct nor immediate. This difficulty does not preclude the achievement of significant insights by considering well-behaved theoretical relationships between expenditures and gift revenues.

Figure 1 shows the simple relationship between fund-raising expenditures and gift revenues for three hypothetical institutions. The bottom line illustrates the relationship for an institution with relatively small returns (and high costs). The middle and top lines illustrate the relationships for institutions with moderate returns (and costs) and large returns (and low costs).

Notice that the lines are different in two respects: their vertical elevation in the figure, and the steepness of their slope from left to right.

The next section proposes separate explanations for these two differences—the elevation of each line and the slope of each line. Subsequent discussions about applications focus on the causal significance and

Figure 1. Simple Relationships

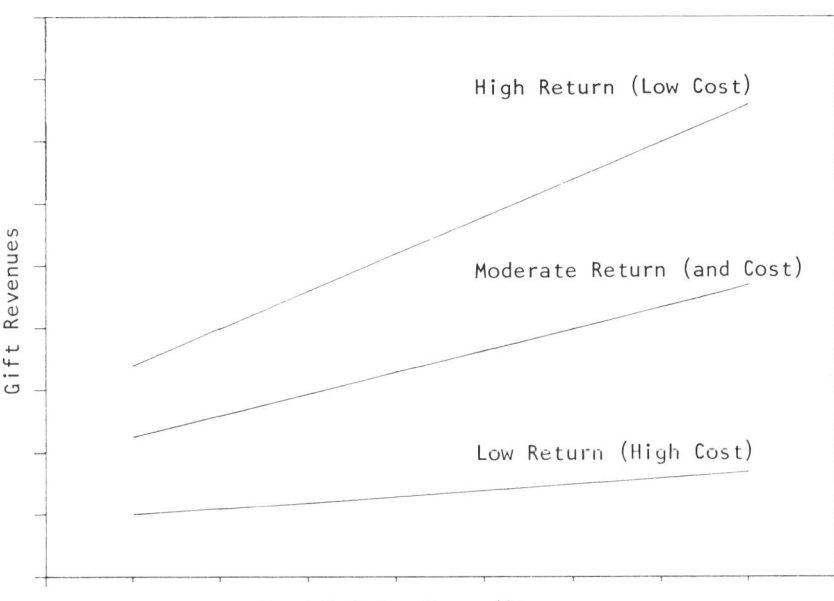

practical implications of these two phenomena. In addition, the discussions introduce conceptual refinements that relax some of the implicit simplifications of Figure 1, for example, the linear depiction of the relationship between expenditures and gift revenues. Most experienced fund raisers know that these lines are not straight. Several other refinements receive attention along the way.

Conceptual Refinements: Predisposition and Capacity

Figure 1 presents the relationship between expenditures and gift revenues as strictly linear throughout the observed range. This simplification ignores two obvious theoretical exceptions to linearity about which fund raisers agree (at least in principle). First, the figure does not illustrate the relationship between expenditures and gift revenues for extremely modest levels of expenditure; in this case, between zero and where the line begins. Second, the figure does not represent the potential limits and increasing difficulty of securing additional giving at higher levels of giving.

This section addresses these two issues by introducing two theoretical concepts that clarify common assertions reflected in the conventional wisdom shared among fund raisers. Resort to these concepts is not a seminal contribution to current thinking, but, rather, a means to explicitly underscore the implicit assumptions and examine more closely some of the practical implications of each.

Effects of Predisposition. Experienced development officers understand that the results of new or very modest fund-raising programs or activities primarily reflect the *a priori* motivation (or willingness) of donor prospects to contribute, independent of efforts to cultivate their support. In rare, but pleasant, instances this motivation precipitates unsolicited giving to a college or university. More often, but not always, *a priori* motivation accounts for a relatively large return of gift revenues (at low costs) for new or modest fund-raising efforts. This return reflects giving by donor prospects for whom the simple fact of being invited to contribute is sufficient to secure a gift.

The potential impact of giving that primarily reflects the strength of prior motivation warrants explicit attention to the concept of donor prospect *predisposition*. The effect of predisposition may be substantial if a large percentage of donor prospects harbor strong motivation to give independently of fund-raising efforts. However, the effect of predisposition may also be insignificant, if few donor prospects are strongly motivated to give in the absence of quite persuasive formal donor prospect cultivation efforts.

Figure 2 compares the relationship between expenditures and gift revenues for an institution with low donor predisposition and another with high predisposition. The slope (steepness from left to right) of the two lines is identical, but the institution with high predisposition receives a larger gift revenue return for the initial level of expenditure shown. The difference is a consequence of the difference in donor prospect predispositions in the two institutions. Strong prior motivation causes a significantly greater response to initial appeals by the institution whose prospects possess higher predisposition.

Predisposition determines the elevation of the line representing the relationship between expenditures and gift revenues. The effect of predisposition is most apparent for modest fund-raising programs consisting of simple appeals for support with little donor prospect cultivation; for example, a general mail appeal program requesting annual contributions. Other less modest fund-raising efforts relying on more extensive and more sophisticated cultivation efforts, such as leadership giving clubs and personal solicitation programs, depend much less on predisposition. These programs attempt to enhance the *a priori* motivation (predisposition) of donor prospects to contribute.

At the lowest levels of expenditure, the relationship between expenditures and gift revenues is quite complicated. Predisposition plays a key role, to be sure, but the start-up costs associated with establishing the minimum level of effective solicitation effort required to capitalize on the

Figure 2. Effect of Predisposition

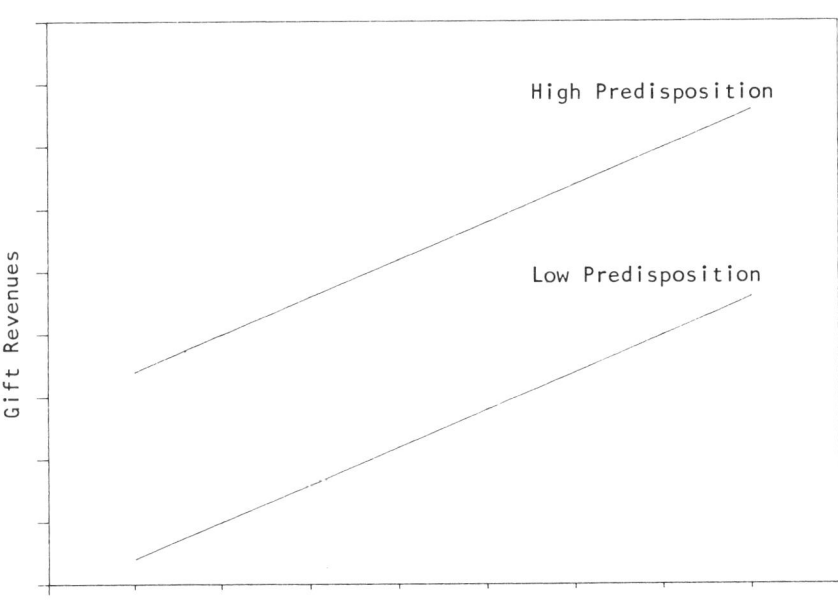

prevailing predisposition is difficult to deduce. The idea of a minimum threshold of fund-raising effort just adequate to secure predisposed giving is intriguing, but exceeds the scope and focus of this chapter.

For this discussion, the important principle is that predisposition determines the elevation of the line representing the relationships between expenditures and gift revenues.

Effects of Capacity. Independent of motivation to give, donor prospect giving *capacity* fundamentally influences the frequency and magnitude of contributions. Development officers freely admit that assumptions about donor wealth and income determine giving prospects and fundraising strategies.

Spectacular capacity overwhelms the importance of predisposition, because the potential for a large contribution justifies the cost of donor prospect relations and cultivation to create motivation if predisposition is low. Low capacity limits the investment that fund raisers are likely to devote to cultivation of an individual donor prospect or group of prospects, because neither predisposition nor induced motivation can secure more than modest support from prospects with limited resources.

Although the exact effect of wealth and income on giving is a matter of some debate, most theoretical models posit an interaction between motivation (reflecting predisposition and donor prospect cultivation) and capacity (reflecting prospect wealth and income). This hypothesized interaction between motivation and capacity is consistent with common economic models of consumer choice, according to which capacity either promotes or inhibits the effect of motivation. This means that the effect of changing motivation depends on giving capacity. Specifically, the gift dollar return that might reasonably be expected to accompany an increase in fund-raising expenditures is determined by the giving capacity of donor prospects.

Figure 3 illustrates a simple case, showing the effect of capacity for two institutions with similar predisposition. The institutions receive similar predisposed gift revenues for similarly modest levels of expenditure for fund raising.

This figure illustrates the consequences of the difference in capacity. First, the returns for increasing levels of expenditure are higher (and the costs lower) for the institution with high capacity than for the institution with low capacity. In addition, although the returns eventually decrease for higher levels of expenditure in both institutions, the level of giving at which this occurs is higher for the institution with high capacity.

This depiction represents capacity as determining the rate of return for fund-raising expenditures. As total giving approaches the theoretical limit of overall capacity for each institution, the return decreases rapidly. Whether or not the relationship between expenditures and gift revenues is strictly or approximately linear above the level of expenditure necessary to

Figure 3. Effects of Capacity

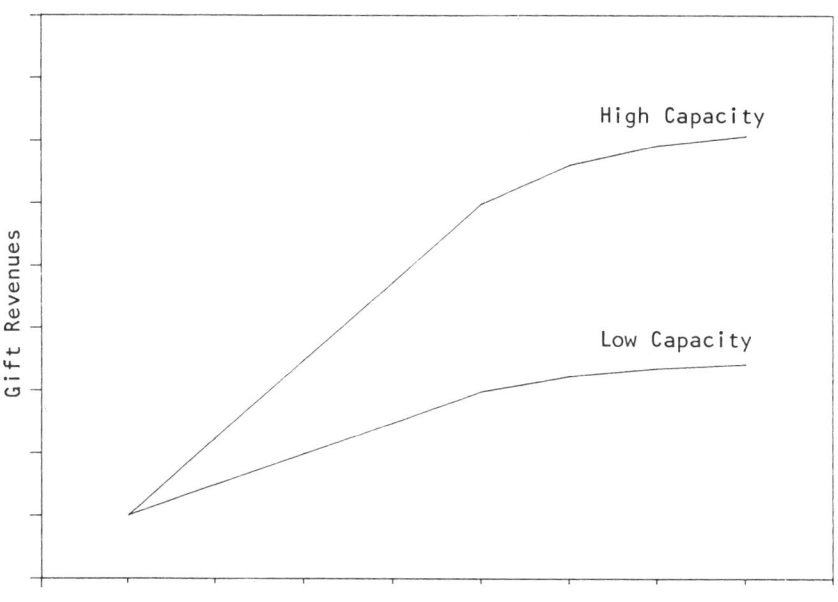

secure predisposed giving and below the level approaching the total theoretical capacity of the donor prospect population is a very important question, but not essential in the current discussion. The line may be curved throughout, slightly at first—with the rate of curvature increasing, rather than linear—and then curved as shown in Figure 3.

Two features of Figure 3 reflect simplifying concessions that may be potentially misleading. Strict adherence to the principle that giving is a joint consequence of motivation (whether predisposed or cultivated) and capacity does not dictate the same amount of predisposed giving for the two institutions if predisposition is the same in both. The level of predisposed giving might actually be higher for the institution with high capacity. In addition, the figure shows the decrease in return starting at the giving level reached via the same level of expenditure in both institutions. This is not necessarily the case, since the level of total giving relative to capacity, not expenditures, determines the region of decreasing return.

The essential principles illustrated in Figure 3 are that capacity determines the slopes of the two lines as well as the levels of giving above which the slopes start to decrease. Donor relations and cultivation efforts can move either institution to higher points of giving on their respective lines, but cannot alter the slopes or the points of decreasing return, which both reflect the giving capacity of the donor prospect population.

Combined Effects. The preceding sections introduce the concepts of donor prospect predisposition and capacity, and describe their impacts on the relationship between fund-raising expenditures and gift revenues. Both factors determine the level of giving that results from investment in fund-raising programs, but the nature of their influence is quite different.

Predisposition determines the magnitude of giving that reflects *a priori* donor motivations sufficient to induce giving in response to modest fund-raising efforts. This impact defines the baseline of giving upon which more ambitious prospect relations and cultivation must build. Capacity determines the rate of return for these more ambitious fund-raising efforts and dictates the limit of total giving near which the return decreases.

Figure 4 illustrates the hypothesized effects of predisposition and capacity in four institutions. The four lines represent the theoretical relationship between expenditures and gift revenues for all four combinations of low or high predisposition and capacity: (1) low predisposition and low capacity, (2) high predisposition and low capacity, (3) low predisposition and high capacity, and (4) high predisposition and high capacity. The starting points for the lines, indicated with crosses (+), show the levels of predisposed giving that occur for modest fund-raising expenditures. The points of decreasing returns for each institution are indicated by solid circles (•).

Figure 4. Predisposition and Capacity: Interactions

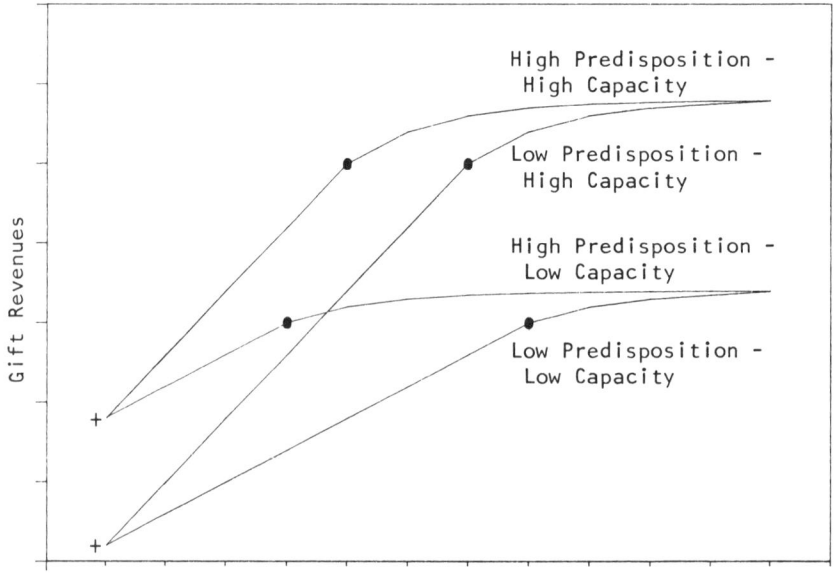

Figure 4 shows the expected consequences of the proposed effects of predisposition and capacity described in this chapter. Note especially the distinction between effects of predisposition and capacity. Predisposition determines the initial return for modest expenditures. Capacity determines the rate of return for additional expenditures exceeding that required to secure predisposed giving, and the level of giving above which this rate of return decreases—as total giving approaches the theoretical capacity of donor prospects.

The practical implications of the relationships shown in Figure 4 are dramatic. Institutions with similar capacity can achieve similar results, but the expenditures required depend directly on the effect of predisposition. Consider that the institution with low predisposition and low capacity must spend approximately twice as much to reach the point of decreasing return as the institution with high predisposition and low capacity. Similarly, the institution with low predisposition and high capacity must spend nearly half again as much as the institution with high predisposition and high capacity to reach the same point.

Perhaps more important, neither institution with low capacity can achieve the maximum results achieved by the institutions with high capacity—at any price. Moreover, in the range of attainable results, institutions with low capacity must pay more to secure giving in excess of predisposed giving than the institutions with high capacity.

The frequent observation about institutions with highly successful fund-raising programs, that "the rich get richer," is consistent with the opportunities or constraints afforded by variation in predisposition and capacity. Some institutions must spend more than others for the gift revenues they can secure, and these revenues may be smaller than for other institutions spending significantly less.

Measuring Costs and Returns. The proposed conceptual bases described in this section provide a critical perspective for understanding and interpreting the results of several efforts to estimate the costs of securing voluntary support among colleges and universities. Before turning to these results in the next section, the short explanation that follows identifies a common distinction between average and marginal costs. This distinction is widely understood but the implications are consistently overlooked in the reported costs studies.

Figure 5 shows the relationship between expenditures and gift revenues for a single institution, along the curved line with points labeled 1 through 10. This depiction resembles previous illustrations, except for the addition of the line from the origin, labeled 0, to point 1. The ten points on the line are labeled 1 through 10, to identify specific levels of expenditures and gift revenues during a ten-year period. For this example, assume that the time period represents the first ten years after the establishment of a new development program in an institution where none existed previously.

Figure 5. Ten Years of Expenditures and Giving

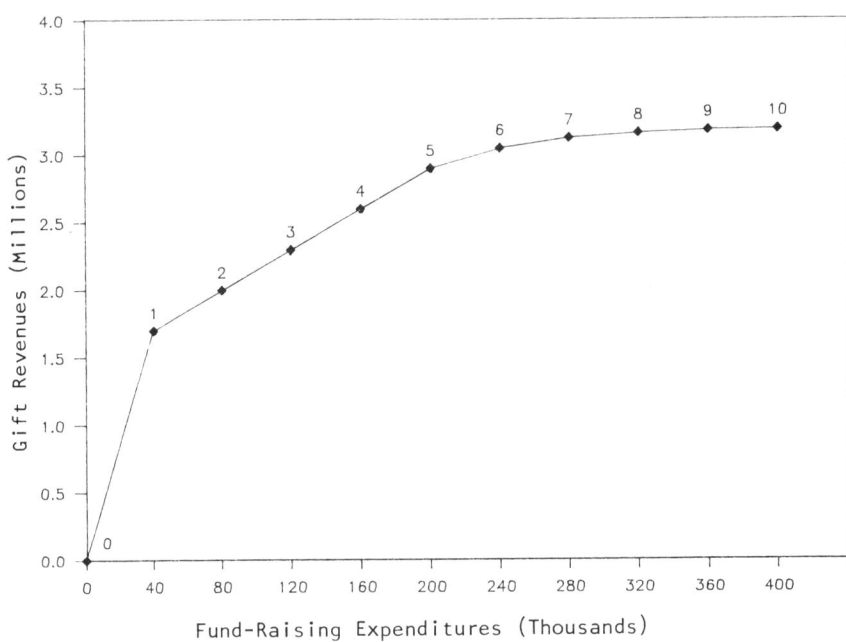

Table 1 displays the values for each point in the figure, together with calculations for average and marginal costs. Consider first the cost of giving in the first year, associated with point 1 on the curve. The cost of these gift revenues is the simple ratio of gift revenues divided by expenditures, that is, $40,000 divided by $1,700,000, or 2.4 cents per gift dollar raised. Note that this is the *average* cost of each of the dollars raised at this level of expenditure. Also recall that this giving, in response to the initial modest effort, includes a high proportion of predisposed giving.

Because the results of the first year are so gratifying, the institution doubles its investment in development during the second year, spending $80,000 altogether. At this higher level of expenditure, the institution receives gift revenues of $2,000,000. The average cost in the second year is $2,000,000 divided by $80,000, or exactly 4.00 cents per dollar raised. The average cost is still quite low, but this average does not tell the whole story.

Comparing the first year to the second underscores the importance of the concept of *marginal* costs, as opposed to average costs. The institution spent $40,000 more in the second year than in the first. For this additional expenditure, the institution received gift revenues $300,000 higher than in the first year. The costs of these additional dollars is $40,000 divided by $300,000, or 13.33 cents per dollar raised. The marginal cost for the incremental gift revenues in the second year is more than three times the average cost for all gifts received that year!

Table 1. Comparing Average Costs and Marginal Costs

Year	Fund-Raising Expenditures	Total Gift Revenues	Average Costs: Expenditures divided by Gift Revenues	Range	Marginal Costs: New Expenditures divided by New Revenues
0	$ 0	$ 0			
1	40,000	1,700,000	$0.024	0-1	$0.024
2	80,000	2,000,000	0.040	1-2	0.133
3	120,000	2,300,000	0.052	2-3	0.133
4	160,000	2,600,000	0.062	3-4	0.133
5	200,000	2,900,000	0.069	4-5	0.133
6	240,000	3,050,000	0.079	5-6	0.267
7	280,000	3,125,000	0.090	6-7	0.533
8	320,000	3,162,500	0.101	7-8	1.067
9	360,000	3,181,250	0.113	8-9	2.133
10	400,000	3,190,625	0.125	9-10	4.267

Notice that the average and marginal costs are the same in year one. This is the case because total expenditures and gift revenues in the first year are the same as new expenditures and gift revenues, since both are zero in the previous year—at least theoretically.

For years 3 through 5, the institution continues to receive $300,000 in additional giving for each $40,000 increase in expenditures. The marginal cost of 13.33 cents is constant throughout this range of giving. Notice that the average cost is increasing in this range, even though the marginal cost is constant. This phenomenon reflects the fact that each succeeding year's receipts include a larger proportion of more expensive gift dollars. In year 1 the total includes $1,700,000 which cost 2.40 cents each. In year 2 the total includes $1,700,000 at 2.40 cents and $300,000 at 13.33 cents. In year 5 the total includes $1,700,000 at 2.40 cents and $1,200,000 at 13.33 cents.

In this example, when giving exceeds $2,900,000 the amount of additional gift revenues received for each $40,000 increase in expenditures declines. This reflects the fact that total giving is approaching the theoretical total capacity of the donor prospect population. In year 6, the increase only nets an additional $150,000, instead of $300,000. In year 8, this increase shrinks to $37,500, for a marginal cost of nearly $1.07 for each additional dollar received. The decline continues through year 10, when the $40,000 increase over year 9 nets less than $10,000 additional gift dollars and the marginal cost is $4.27 for each dollar raised! But the average cost is still only 12.50 cents per dollar raised. This average is obviously quite misleading.

The distinction between average and marginal costs is particularly important for monitoring the efficiency of fund-raising effects, because the impact of a potentially high proportion of low-cost predisposed giving in the total tends to obscure less-efficient performance at the margin. This tendency invites seriously misleading expectations about incremental giving likely to accompany increased expenditures. The mistake can be very expensive.

Although employed less frequently in the professional literature, the concepts of average and marginal *returns* underscore the same features of the relationship between fund-raising expenditures and gift revenues as average and marginal costs. Table 2 reports the average and marginal returns that correspond to the costs reported in Table 1.

Notice that, within the limits of rounding errors, the corresponding costs in Table 1 and returns in Table 2 are reciprocals of one another. For example, the average cost of exactly 4.00 cents in year 2 is equivalent to 1/25th of a dollar spent per gift dollar raised. Equivalently, the average return in the year 2 is $25 in gift revenues per dollar spent.

The returns reported in Table 2 are equivalent to the patterns of costs reported in Table 1. The average and marginal returns are the same in year 1; in years 2 through 5, the marginal returns are constant but lower than in year 1, and the average returns are decreasing; in years 6 through 10, the marginal returns decrease rapidly while the average returns decrease more slowly. The average returns after year 8 do not reveal that the marginal return is less than $1 for each dollar spent.

Table 2. Comparing Average Returns and Marginal Returns

Year	Fund-Raising Expenditures	Total Gift Revenues	Average Returns: Gift Revenues divided by Expenditures	Range	Marginal Returns: New Revenues divided by New Expenditures
0	$ 0	$ 0			
1	40,000	1,700,000	$42.50	0-1	$42.50
2	80,000	2,000,000	25.00	1-2	7.50
3	120,000	2,300,000	19.17	2-3	7.50
4	160,000	2,600,000	16.25	3-4	7.50
5	200,000	2,900,000	14.50	4-5	7.50
6	240,000	3,050,000	12.71	5-6	3.75
7	280,000	3,125,000	11.16	6-7	1.88
8	320,000	3,162,500	9.88	7-8	0.94
9	360,000	3,181,250	8.84	8-9	0.47
10	400,000	3,190,625	7.98	9-10	0.23

Research Estimating the Costs of Fund Raising

Of the handful of formal efforts to estimate development costs for individual institutions, results of the seminal work and subsequent follow-ups by John Leslie (1969; 1971; 1977) are the most widely disseminated. Summary data from a similar study conducted by the Consortium on Financing Higher Education (COFHE) have been reported (Ramsden, 1979), but details of the data remain the exclusive property of the COFHE member institutions (COFHE, 1976). The Council for the Advancement of Small Colleges (CASC) maintains a data analysis service, which administers a Fund-Raising Module for monitoring measures of development performance, including costs per gift dollar (CASC, 1979). However, the data accumulated from colleges that purchase the data service have not been reported publicly.

Small groups of institutions occasionally cooperate to share informally information about development performance. Once such effort was organized by James Ridenour (1978) at Western Maryland College, to assemble data from a sample of colleges in the region. More recently, John Dunn has spearheaded a similar plan to assemble development data from approximately twenty-five private universities. The results of preliminary efforts to examine similar data from a subset of these institutions have been reported (Dunn and Adam, 1985).

These systematic attempts to examine the performance of development efforts and the costs of securing support employ relatively similar definitions and methods. The consistencies that prevail probably reflect the standardizing influence of the annual survey of voluntary support conducted by the Council for Financial Aid to Education (CFAE) more than any conscious effort to use similar definitions among the studies. Data from the survey have been reported by CFAE each year since the middle 1960s in their annual report, *Voluntary Support of Education* (CFAE, 1966–1984). The survey and report afford a *de facto* standard for defining gift revenues received by colleges and universities, and the cost studies approximately define as fund-raising expenditures those devoted to securing CFAE gift revenues.

Relatively minor differences among the cost studies reflect various smoothing strategies for representing gift revenues received via bequests and various trust or annuity arrangements. Since giving in these categories is often quite volatile from year to year, reflecting occasionally very large individual contributions, some of the studies employ three- or five-year averages to represent these components of total gift revenues. Other studies exclude bequests and trusts from the total.

Bequests, trusts and annuities, and other very large contributions pose a special problem for monitoring costs, because such gifts often reflect several years of ongoing donor prospect relations and cultivation efforts.

In addition, bequests are particularly troublesome, because the timing of the actual receipt of the gift is an actuarial event largely independent of the extent and timing of fund-raising efforts.

For larger development operations with mature major gift, bequest, and deferred giving programs, these difficulties are less serious. For newer or more modest operations, conduct of these giving programs requires current expenditures for donor prospect relations and cultivation that are *investments* for future gift revenues.

Most of the cost studies warn that the fund-raising expenditures recorded probably underestimate the full costs of giving, because some institutional programs and activities that support fund raising are executed outside the development office, so expenses for these appear in other than development budgets. Leslie includes expenditures for public relations, alumni affairs, and publications, together with direct expenditures for fund-raising activities. In contrast, the COFHE and CASC methods are more selective, including all expenses for direct fund-raising activities but only those public relations, alumni affairs, and publications expenses that are for activities that directly support fund-raising.

None of the studies attempts to include expenses associated with the time devoted to development by senior academic officers, faculty, or others. The central importance of the president's participation in development, for example, certainly justifies the concept that a portion of his or her salary is a legitimate fund-raising expense. Other senior administrative officers or deans probably participate in development activities too, though less extensively. Few institutions routinely monitor the expense of such personnel time devoted to development. Whether or not the effort to do so is worth the trouble is certainly debatable.

Consistency in recording fund-raising expenditures among institutions for comparative purposes is far more important than an absolutely comprehensive accounting, in any case. On this point, the several cost studies that have been conducted afford reasonably reliable data.

Estimated Costs. Table 3 summarizes the fund-raising costs estimated in the studies identified above. The table also indicates the date of each study (or time period covered), together with the number and description of institutions included. The range of estimated fund-raising costs and approximate median are reported for each study.

Despite wide variation in the costs observed in each study, and significant differences among types of institutions, the medians reported for individual types that appear in more than one study are remarkably similar. The medians for costs reported for private universities in three studies conducted exactly eight years apart are grouped between 7 and 9 cents. The actual distributions of reported costs (not shown) reveal that the majority are between 5 cents and 20 cents.

Costs of giving among private colleges are slightly less narrowly dis-

Table 3. Selected Studies of Expenditures per Gift Dollar Raised

Type and Number of Institutions	Study	Approximate Timing of Data Collection	Expenditures per Gift Dollar (Cents) Range	Median
Private Colleges				
N=72	Leslie	(1969)[a]	6-99	19
N=71	CASC	(early 1970s)		18[b]
N=10	Ridenour	(1978)		17[b]
N=11	COFHE	(1976)	5-18	7
Private Universities				
N=12	Leslie	(1969)[a]	5-42	9
N=14	COFHE	(1976)	4-11	7
N=10	Dunn	(1984)	4-28	8
Public Universities				
N=19	Leslie	(1969)[a]	7-132	20

[a] Similar results reported from follow-up studies in 1971 and 1977.
[b] Reported average is the mean for costs, not the median.

tributed, but this variation requires an explanatory comment. The COFHE sample of private colleges is a very homogenous group of the most highly selective, elite liberal arts colleges in the country. These colleges have among the most mature, stable, and ambitious development programs of any liberal arts colleges. The relatively narrow range of costs observed in this group, from a low of 5 cents to a high of 18 cents, reflects the maturity and stability of these programs as well as the similarities among these colleges.

In sharp contrast to the COFHE group, the private colleges in the Leslie and CASC samples are much less alike, both in the magnitude, nature, and maturity of development efforts, as well as general college characteristics such as size, selectivity, educational mission, and curricular emphasis. A significant percentage of the colleges in both studies, but particularly in the CASC sample, are very small, unselective, regional or local colleges. A large number of these colleges confronted serious financial challenges during the time of the cost studies, and many were pursuing (for them) relatively ambitious strategies to expand previously modest development programs. The colleges in the Ridenour sample are more similar to the Leslie and CASC groups than to the COFHE group. The Leslie, CASC, and Ridenour cost estimates for private colleges are all between 18 and 24 cents.

The only cost estimates for public universities are from the Leslie sample. This limited base of evidence indicates very dramatic variation from lowest to highest costs, from 7 cents to one dollar and 32 cents, with the median at 20 cents. The reliability of these figures is difficult to evaluate, because the sample is small and old. If publicly reported gift revenues are any indication, the nature and magnitude of development efforts among public institutions have undergone profound changes during the last two decades. Since the middle 1960s, the percentage of all voluntary support of higher education received by public four-year institutions has approximately doubled, from less than 15 percent of the total to more than 30 percent (CFAE, 1966–1984). This dramatic change is a very good reason to interpret the Leslie data with some reservation.

Practical Application: Interpreting Costs

The most important reminder regarding all of the studies of fund-raising costs per gift dollar is that they examine *average* costs, not marginal costs. This point warrants repeating. The costs reported in Table 3 are average costs, not marginal costs. In every case, the cost estimates for individual institutions are determined by dividing total fund-raising expenditures by total gift revenues.

The comparisons between average and marginal costs in the previous section underscore the potential pitfalls of exclusive reliance on average costs as an indicator of fund-raising performance. Average cost estimates for institutions with very modest or relatively new (immature) development operations are likely to be the least reliable indicators of future performance, because gift revenues among these institutions include higher percentages of low-cost predisposed giving.

Except for general observations about probable pressures to increase voluntary support in response to financial jeopardy, and the obvious maturity of development programs among the COFHE institutions, nothing is known about the context and status of fund-raising efforts among individual colleges and universities in the cost studies. Certainly some of the programs are relatively new, receiving substantial predisposed giving. Costs among these institutions would be atypically low.

No doubt, many of the institutions were in the midst of building to higher levels of support for the future; that is, investing current fund-raising expenditures for future gift income—as a hedge against deteriorating prospects for tuition and other, revenues. Costs in these institutions should be expected to be atypically high. Acute financial crises among some institutions may have actually precipitated short-term decreases in development expenditures, to preserve budget support for academic programs. Average costs in such cases could be lower than normal, reflecting the momentum of previous investment in fund raising which is not being replaced.

These idiosyncrasies obscured beneath the simple estimates of average costs require explicit consideration for realistic interpretation of fund-raising performance. Despite these warnings, the results of cost studies provide valuable normative benchmarks for identifying realistic development expectations and monitoring the effectiveness of ongoing fund-raising programs and activities.

The available evidence indicates a range of typical average costs among private universities between 5 cents and 20 cents, with costs in stable mature development programs between 5 and 10 cents, and in developing or expanding programs between 10 and 20 cents. Average costs below this range probably reflect very modest programs receiving primarily predisposed giving, or temporarily low costs reflecting the momentum of previous development investments rather than current effort—that is, capital consumption without replacement.

In private colleges, the typical range for average costs is between 10 cents and 25 cents, with costs in stable mature programs between 10 and 15 cents, and in developing or expanding efforts between 15 and 25 cents. Average costs below 10 cents suggest a large proportion of primarily predisposed giving or temporary consumption of prior investments.

Among these several cost studies, the average costs reported by institutions receiving the largest volume of voluntary support (not shown here) are consistently in the middle or slightly lower than the middle of the reported cost ranges. This finding is preliminary evidence that the most successful development operations are not experiencing dramatically high costs that would accompany giving levels close to exhausting total donor prospect capacity.

Capital Investment and Consumption. Temporary development "profit-taking" is analogous to the short-term corporate financial strategies about which many business analysts have recently been critical. Executing closure on major gift prospects cultivated via lengthy donor relations efforts over a period of years without continuing to cultivate new major gift prospects for the long-term future; waiting for mortality to deliver previously established bequest commitments without pursuing new bequest prospects; focusing on the remaining few of the top priority donor prospects identified by the most recent comprehensive prospect research and screening effort *ten years ago* rather than conducting a new prospecting effort—all of these behaviors are dangerous forms of capital consumption, not unlike the corporate capital consumption responsible for the dilapidated facilities and equipment or obsolete production processes in corporate manufacturing.

This strategy may afford artificially low average fund-raising costs on a short-term basis, but the efficiency is illusory. To sustain giving levels, the long-term investments in prospect research and cultivation, volunteer networks, and other fund-raising capital must be replaced eventually. Atypically low costs probably reflect postponed expense, not real efficiencies. Moreover, depleting and recreating these investments may be more expensive than maintaining them on an ongoing basis. Stopping and starting basic research and development, in development as in industry, is expensive. Recent recognition of this may be partly responsible for the trend toward fund-raising strategies of continuous campaigning among some of the most consistently successful development operations.

Research About Predisposition and Capacity. The majority of other research about development efforts reflects the nearly exclusive prescriptive emphasis of the professional development literature. Many studies examine the relative effectiveness of alternative fund-raising practices, in an attempt to identify optimal strategies and techniques. However, these studies confront the common frustration of limited knowledge and understanding about relevant institutional differences that promote or inhibit the productivity of fund-raising efforts, independent of the effectiveness of the specific techniques employed.

John Leslie (1979) presents a perceptive case for the need to better understand the role and impact of institutional differences, under the heading of estimating gift *potential*. Leslie summarizes the need succinctly:

> "How well did we do compared to how well we could have done?" This question should be on the lips of every college and university fund-raising manager. It suggests a driving desire to achieve potential—to wring every ounce of productivity out of every dollar that the institution spends on people and support funds in an effort to secure private gifts. But assessing annual fund-raising potential and developing reliable measurements are not simple tasks. Potentials vary from one institution to another, and (at least at the present moment) no standard system is available. This fact, however, does not negate the importance of dollar-potential assessment in the effective management of education fund-raising programs [p. 59].

This affirmation of the value of knowing and understanding the impact of gift potential acknowledges the difficulty of identifying systematic methods to do so. The major obstacle is the difficulty of assessing donor prospect predisposition and capacity as described in this chapter. The methods for evaluating predisposition and capacity are so far largely subjective and qualitative—relying on the experienced intuitions of the directors and managers of development programs. In the absence of formal theoretical bases and practical methods for making more objective quantitative assessments, the professional literature focuses on simple relationships between fund-raising expenditures and gift revenues. Leslie continues: ["N]o broad-based study of fund-raising potential is listed in the literature of the field or known to the author. Rather, the principal focus of research to date has been along the lines of attempting to measure efficiency—dollars spent versus dollars raised" (1979, p. 60).

The content of the professional literature has not changed dramatically since Leslie's summary of research needs seven years ago. Most published material still begs the question of donor potential and variation in potential among different institutions and different types of institutions.

The limited progress of current research about institutional differences which influence predisposition and capacity underscores the value and importance of internal research to monitor development performance within institutions. Institutional monitoring of the relationship between expenditures and gift revenues is the best current source of information for strategic planning and ongoing management of program effectiveness.

Systematic institutional research to estimate marginal costs of gift revenues or returns to fund-raising expenditures is also an essential prerequisite to improve the availability of reliable data for examining the impacts of institutional characteristics on predisposition and capacity. Comparative research cannot achieve significant progress until record keeping practices improve *within* institutions.

The traditionally low priority of efforts to monitor costs or returns within individual development offices is not surprising. In the absence of reliable comparative norms for estimating realistic resource requirements to achieve development objectives, many development offices confront ambitious expectations far in excess of reasonable staff capacities. This phenomenon forces a desperate trade-off of personnel time between getting the impossible job done and conducting institutional research about the productivity of the effort. The cycle is vicious, and research is the consistent loser. This is not a minor irony.

The Utility of Gift Revenues. Justifying the costs of securing voluntary support requires fundamentally different judgments than simple comparison to typical norms. Identifying a realistic range of expectations for voluntary support, and estimating likely resource requirements for pursuing these expectations are primarily technical exercises. In contrast, establishment of specific goals and commitment of resources for achieving them requires highly qualitative judgments.

Most fund raisers explicitly understand that different kinds of gift revenues have different value. Unrestricted giving has the highest utility, because this income can be used for any purpose. Restricted giving for purposes currently supported by unrestricted revenues from nondevelopment sources (for example, tuition revenues) has the next highest utility. This restricted giving releases unrestricted revenues from other sources for reassignment—the net effect is the same as for unrestricted giving. The utility of giving for other restricted purposes is a direct function of the priority of the specific purposes and the availability of alternative methods for financing them.

This common understanding about the differential utility of different kinds of gift revenues is a fundamental consideration in justifying fund-raising costs. Even more important, however, overall financial circumstances of individual institutions are critical determinants of justifiable fund-raising costs. Within the broad limits of publicly defensible cost ranges, institutions may elect to endure relatively high costs of voluntary support temporarily, to confront immediate financial urgencies. Quantitative studies that examine simple costs of giving or returns to fund-raising expenditures obscure these important justifications. No doubt, this limitation of quantitative measures contributes to understandable defensiveness about public disclosure of costs or returns.

Non-Incremental Development Alternatives. The preceding discussion focuses on the dynamics of incremental changes in development strategies. It examines relationships between development expenditures and gift revenues for traditional donor prospect constituencies, primarily including prospects identified via formal affiliation to a specific institution (as with alumni), or via a presumed interest in the institution (as with local corporations or foundations with stated agendas to support higher education). The discussion of effects of predisposition and capacity presented here implicitly assumes that the total donor prospect population, reflecting tangible prospect affiliations and interests, is a fixed institutional resource, subject only to slow marginal evolutions over extended time periods. Recent evidence reveals development strategies that challenge this traditional assumption.

A handful of institutions have recently achieved notable successes by pursuit of gift support from prospects outside traditionally defined constituencies, particularly including major gift prospects with little or no previous affiliation to the institution. These efforts represent a special case of the relationships examined here, in which the alluring potential of spectacular capacity justifies development activity despite minimal or nonexistent predisposition. The results of these efforts are predictable. With little or no predisposed giving, returns for modest investment in this strategy are low. However, the prospect of potentially spectacular benefactions justifies the cost and risk of this development strategy, particularly if the results of efforts with other constituencies are constrained by modest residual capacity at current giving levels.

The typical costs and effectiveness of this departure from traditional development practice are not well understood, but the strategy reveals a potential hedge against the fundamental constraint of donor prospect capacity. Although development efforts cannot alter the capacity of individual prospects, donor prospect research can identify high-capacity prospects outside the traditional constituencies. Highly focused prospect relations and cultivation efforts with these new potential donors may prove to be an effective alternative to pursuit of marginal improvements in support from current constituencies.

Looking to the Future

Although the ideas discussed in this chapter are not new to fund raisers, theoretical bases and research methods to confirm and refine practical interpretations and applications of these concepts are not currently well developed. On the bright side, recent activity among the professional associations reflects a growing impetus to devote attention to systematic research about fund raising and giving, based on common standards and definitions for recording and reporting information about the performance of development programs.

The cooperative effort by the Council for Advancement and Support of Education (CASE) and the National Association of College and University Business Officers (NACUBO), to establish common reporting standards for gift revenues and fund-raising expenditures is a significant contribution. Within CASE, the recent appointment of a national committee to review research needs and recommend strategies to promote academic and applied inquiries examining theoretical and conceptual bases of the development enterprise is a promising commitment to improving research methods.

The continuing progress of research to understand development performance directly depends upon the improvement of efforts to gather performance data *within* institutions. Normative comparisons to identify typical costs and returns for different types of institutions and different development strategies and techniques require the accumulation of comparable data consistently reported by a large number of colleges and universities.

The identification of straightforward procedures for estimating expenditures attributable to development programs and activities is crucial. No other single accomplishment will improve research about development so much as identification of *practical* methods for monitoring development expenditures routinely. Of necessity, the evolution of monitoring efforts must begin modestly. The trade-off between praticality and methodological perfection and comprehensiveness is critical. Reasonably consistent approximations for expenditures among one hundred institutions are far more valuable than perfect detail for five.

As data collection methods improve and the general level of understanding about development performance becomes more sophisticated, subsequent inquiries will pursue refinements to estimate the impact of specific conditions and circumstances associated with variation in costs or returns among different institutions. In the meantime, internal research monitoring changes in average and marginal costs *within* individual institutions is the only realistic method for planning and managing effective performance.

References

Consortium on Financing Higher Education. *A Comparative Study of Development and University Relations at Twenty-Five Colleges and Universities.* Hanover, N.H.: COFHE, 1976.

Council for Financial Aid to Education, Division of Research. *Voluntary Support of Education* (Nineteen annual volumes). New York: CFAE, 1965-1966 through 1983-84.

Council for the Advancement of Small Colleges. Unpublished report for subscribers to the CASC Planning and Data System Fund-Raising Module (prepared by Minter Associates), 1979.

Dunn, J. A., Jr., and Adam, A. "Fund-Raising Costs and Staffing: A Comparison of Ten Private Universities, 1985." Paper presented to the NEAIR Annual Conference, Hartford, Conn., 1985.

Leslie, J. W. *Focus on Understanding and Support: A Study in College Management.* Washington, D.C.: American College Public Relations Association, 1969.

Leslie, J. W. "Seeking the Competitive Dollar: College Management in the Seventies." *College and University Journal*, Nov. 1971, pp. 3-57.

Leslie, J. W. Unpublished memorandum to responders to the Institutional Advancement Management Survey, March 11, 1977.

Leslie, J. W. "Variations in Fund-Raising Potential Among Colleges and Universities." In W. Heemann (ed.), *Analyzing the Cost Effectiveness of Fund Raising.* New Directions for Institutional Advancement, no. 3. San Francisco: Jossey-Bass, 1979.

Ramsden, R. J. "The COFHE Development Study: Insights and Implications." In W. Heemann (ed.), *Analyzing the Cost Effectiveness of Fund Raising.* New Directions for Institutional Advancement, no. 3. San Francisco: Jossey-Bass, 1979.

Ridenour, J. F. Unpublished report. Westminster, Md.: Office of Development, Western Maryland College, August 9, 1978.

G. Jeffry Paton is an assistant professor of educational administration at the University of Rochester. He is currently on temporary leave from teaching to serve as director of Development Planning and Administration and as special assistant to the Office of the President.

Comparing your institution's fund-raising cash proceeds with those of other colleges and universities is straightforward, given CFAE data. Measuring fund-raising productivity, however, requires care in defining related expenses and resulting fund-raising achievements. Simplifying assumptions can be helpful.

Comparative Studies of Fund-Raising Performance

John A. Dunn, Jr., Dawn Geronimo Terkla, Audrey Adam

It is surprising that so few comparative studies of fund raising have been carried out. The dollars raised are important to their recipients; the activity (at least the annual fund portion of it) is cyclical, so that trends can easily be traced; and, through the good graces of the Council for Financial Aid to Education (CFAE), reasonably good data on achievements are collected annually on most higher education institutions and independent secondary schools in the United States.

Such studies could address important management questions. How effective is our college's or university's fund raising in comparison to similar institutions? (For the question of how are we doing versus our own potential, see Chapter Two on fund-raising theory.) How much are we spending per dollar raised? Can we allocate fund-raising resources more effectively?

This chapter suggests ways of structuring studies of fund-raising *proceeds* (cash receipts) and then goes on to the more difficult questions of comparing performance on fund-raising *progress* (cash and pledges), associated expenditures, and productivity. Data on proceeds are readily available, and lend themselves to straightforward analysis. Here we simply suggest questions for study. With respect to fund-raising progress, expenditures, and productivity, however, there are far more uncertainties. We therefore present in the latter part of the chapter a more structured case study of a "Sample University."

The essence of the approach we suggest is to gather the information needed in any case for proper management of the development activity, and to compare on that basis. Each of the procedures and tables given here lends itself to year-to-year analysis of your own institution, as well as to multi-institution comparisons. We suggest that analysis, like charity, should begin at home.

Fund-Raising Proceeds

In general, development officers would like to be judged by their total fund-raising progress, including not only outright gifts but also pledges and deferred gift intentions secured during the year. Achieving a clear definition of "progress," however, raises a variety of sticky questions, which will be dealt with later in this chapter.

In its annual surveys entitled *Voluntary Support of Education*, CFAE takes the enormously simplifying step of requesting institutions to report only their actual fund-raising proceeds—that is, the cash (and cash value of gifts in kind) they received during the year. CFAE asks that its survey be completed in November for the previous academic year, and generally is able to publish its annual report late the following spring.

Researchers may want to check institutionally supplied CFAE data against Higher Education General Information Survey (HEGIS) or other official records, in such areas as enrollments, endowment, and educational and general budgets. The CFAE figures in these areas sometimes differ significantly from those separately reported on HEGIS or other surveys.

In recent years, the data published in *Voluntary Support for Education* have included the following:
- total private support
- support for current operations, unrestricted and restricted
- capital support, by purpose
- sources of support: individuals, corporations, foundations, and so on
- forms of giving: bequests, and so on
- annual fund support, including numbers of alumni and of alumni donors
- gifts of property
- corporate matching gifts.

Additional data collected by CFAE but not published (at least not through 1983-84) include the following:
- trustee giving

- number and value of gifts over $5000
- value of three highest individual, corporate, and foundation gifts
- number of donors and value of gifts from students, faculty and staff, and parents.

Eager researchers can ask their comparison-group colleagues to exchange their CFAE submissions directly, thus getting somewhat more complete data several months before publication.

Simplifying Assumptions. For many analyses of overall fund-raising performance, it is useful to ignore the distinction between gifts for current and capital purposes. Fund raisers can influence the distribution of gifts between these categories to some extent, asking donors for one kind of gift or another. It is the total dollars raised that is often of most interest.

You may also wish to disregard whether particular institutions in your sample are engaged in capital campaigns. Several years ago, capital campaigns were more clearly distinguishable from "ordinary" fund raising, with longer time periods between campaigns, and with significantly enhanced personnel and expenditures during campaign periods. Nowadays, many institutions are always in campaign mode; whether or not they declare a "campaign" depends on their marketing strategy.

Achievement Measures. The simplest fund-raising achievement measures are (1) total dollars raised and (2) total dollars raised in relation to institutional expenditures. If you are comparing institutions of different sizes or wealth, the total dollars measure will typically favor the larger, longer lived, and wealthier. A more useful measure in that case is fund-raising "leverage," an index of how important fund raising is to the institution, or, put another way, an index of how well the institution is doing for its size. This second measure is derived by dividing total dollars raised by an institutional expenditures measure such as educational and general expenditures plus mandatory transfers, or total expenditures and transfers.

Note that "fund-raising leverage" is a crude measure, in which the numerator contains operating as well as capital gifts, but the denominator represents only operating expenditures. Sometimes, however, vigorous analysis is more helpful than rigorous.

An alternative "leverage" measure can be derived, of course, by dividing total dollars raised by number of students. For comparing nonresearch-oriented schools, this format may be useful. For universities with substantial research and service activities, it is a less useful indicator.

You can compare institutions on their success with respect to operating funds or capital funds raised; on their gifts from various sources, and in various forms; and on their annual fund gifts.

Participation Rates and Average Gift Sizes. A second series of analyses involves looking at the number and value of gifts from individuals, especially in terms of the size of the potential constituency.

Alumni constitute the traditional base for giving, especially for annual operating support. The most useful measures here are participation rates (alumni annual fund donors/alumni of record); average gift size (total alumni annual fund dollars/alumni annual fund donors); and per capita support (total annual fund dollars from alumni/alumni of record). Alumni of record is not a perfect measure of the size of the alumni/ae constituency, since it omits those living alumni for whom the institution has no mailing address. Nonetheless, it is more useful in an understanding of the institution's overall performance than other divisors such as alumni solicited or alumni who have given at some time or alumni ten years or more after graduation.

To see how vigorously gifts are sought, you can calculate the number of alumni solicited as a percentage of alumni of record. You can then judge the effectiveness of the solicitation in two ways: check the percentage of solicited alumni who actually gave; and calculate the size of the average gift from alumni donors.

You will want to look also at capital gifts from alumni. CFAE collects data on number of alumni giving for all purposes as well as the number giving to the annual fund. Unfortunately, it is not possible to see how many alumni gave to both, so one cannot derive a pure number of alumni donors for capital purposes. By taking the simplifying assumption of combining operating and capital gifts, it is possible (and useful) to calculate total alumni dollars per alumnus of record, the percentage of alumni of record giving for all purposes, and average total alumni gift size (total dollars from alumni/total alumni donors.)

It is well to remember that alumni are not the only present or potential donors. CFAE collects data on gifts from parents and from other individuals as well as from alumni. It is interesting to check average gift sizes from these constituencies, and to calculate what portion of total giving comes from them. These populations, as well as corporations and foundations, are particularly important to new colleges and universities and to those that, while older, are new to aggressive fund raising.

Dependence on Large Gifts and on Trustees. Starting in 1983-84, CFAE collected data on the number and value of gifts from trustees, of all gifts over $5000, and on the dollar value of the institution's three largest gifts each from individuals, foundations, and corporations. When taken together with the achievement and participation measures described above, these data elements now allow you to calculate the extent to which your institution is dependent on a few large donors. These considerations are of special importance in thinking ahead about future fund-raising possibilities. An old rule of thumb was that a significant percentage (15 to 40 percent, depending on campaign size) of an independent institution's capital campaign had to come from its own governing board(s), if the campaign were to be successful. This may no longer hold true, but board leadership is still of critical importance.

Trend Analyses. Fund raisers will sometimes correctly point out that scrutiny of fund-raising proceeds in a single year can be misleading. A small number of major gifts or bequests that happen to mature that year can indeed make year-to-year comparisons seem discontinuous. For this reason, trend analyses are particularly useful.

Each of the indicators identified above can and should be plotted over time. Simple regressions against time can smooth out bumpy annual figures, and give you a sense of the direction and magnitude of progress. You may even, depending on the confidence you have in your data, and the number of years you have, want to see whether your trends are curvilinear rather than straight.

Trends at your own institution can then be plotted, and can be compared with similiar trends at competing or similar institutions. Average annual percentage growth rates are useful indicators.

Fund-Raising Progress

The cash proceeds realized last year often represent development efforts of preceding years, especially with respect to bequests realized or large gifts that took years to solicit and years to pay out. Not surprisingly, most development personnel would prefer to be judged on their current performance. Moreover, if we are to do any productivity studies of development operations, the current expenses must be linked in some fashion with current success in signing up donors.

No organization we know of collects data on fund-raising progress. Any study you undertake that needs these figures will have to be tailor-made for your own purposes. In deciding what to count in fund-raising progress, you will have to be explicit with respect to the exclusion of payments on prior-year pledges, and with respect to the inclusion of new outright gifts, new pledges, and new deferred gift intentions.

Difficulties include valuation of gifts to be made in the future, and inclusion of testamentary commitments. Does one count $1,000,000 to be paid over seven years as representing the same "progress" as $1,000,000 to be paid now? How does one distinguish between the executed will of a person who is clearly not going to survive the night, and the executed will of a sixty-year-old just married for the seventh time? Universities with medical schools and hospitals may have a specially difficult problem with associated fund raising from grateful patients.

The guidelines issued by the Council for Advancement and Support of Education and the National Association of College and University Business Officers (see Chapter Two) are of great help in dealing with some of these questions, but the inclusion of testamentary commitments in calculations of fund-raising progress (disallowed under those guidelines) remains controversial.

In looking at fund-raising proceeds, you will want to examine both the range of gift sizes, the sources of those gifts, and the form (bequests, and so on). As pointed out in Chapter One, most fund-raising planning is based on some projected "giving table" that indicates, from experience, that you will need to receive a few huge gifts, a reasonable number of large gifts, a quantity of moderate gifts, and a great number of small gifts in order to make your goal. Gifts of all sizes will be sought from all sources and in all forms, though small gifts are typically sought only from individuals, and many huge gifts come in the form of bequests.

Fund-raising organizations typically staff their efforts accordingly. They have individuals working on the small gifts, usually through an annual fund; other focusing on moderate gifts; and a few key people working full-time on the "huge-gift" prospects. In addition, they have experts working on corporation, foundation, and deferred gifts.

The point to be made here is to organize the data on fund-raising proceeds so that they can be related to the staffing in the organization that is seeking the gifts. Table 1 shows one way of categorizing fund-raising progress.

If your comparison group can agree to organize their data in this or some similar format, you can then compare progress, overall, and by sources, forms, and gift sizes.

Fund-Raising Expenditures

If you are interested mainly in tracking changes in your own institution's fund-raising expenditures, you can follow whatever organizational definitions make best sense to you. However, since development organizations differ significantly, it is well to start out with a careful definition of what is to be included or excluded.

Several suggestions may be helpful in that delineation:

Include all costs of fund raising and development and associated support personnel, but exclude personnel and costs associated with alumni relations, community relations, and public relations unless they have a bottom-line responsibility for fund raising.

Exclude the time and associated costs of the president, provost, deans and others. They may be your best fund raisers, but they should be included only if (and to the extent that) their offices would not exist except for their fund-raising role. For example, you would include a school's associate dean whose job is to work on fund raising, but exclude the school dean, who would be there in any case.

Include applicable computing costs, whether they are incurred in the development office or in the computing center.

Include the cost of fund-raising publications, such as case statements, solicitation letters, and the like, but exclude regular alumni newsletters and other publications.

Table 1. Fund-Raising Progress[a] at Sample University, FY 19XX

	Corporations and Corporate Foundations[b]		Foundations and Associations		Individuals — Alumni/ae		Individuals — Non-alumni/ae		TOTAL	
Gift Size Range	No.	(Thousands)	No.	(Thousands)	No.	(Thousands)	No.	(Thousands)	No.	(Thousands)
1. $5,000,000 up	0	0	0	0	0	0	0	0	0	0
2. 1,000,000 up	0	0	0	0	1	1500	0	0	1	1500
3. 500,000 up	3	1900	4	2200	2	1100	1	500	10	5700
4. 100,000 up	10	1900	9	1875	6	725	5	730	30	5230
5. 50,000 up	10	750	12	875	5	337	2	150	29	2112
6. 10,000 up	14	795	15	600	24	550	15	440	68	2385
7. 5,000 up	25	203	15	120	20	160	12	85	72	568
8. Under $5,000	xxxxx	370	xxxxx	200	xxxxx	3200	xxxxx	750	xxxxx	4520
9. Corporate matching	xxxxx	xxxxx	xxxxx	xxxxx	xxxxx	400	xxxxx	75	xxxxx	475
10. Subtotal		5918		5870		7972		2730		22490
11. Testamentary Commitments	xxxxx	xxxxx	xxxxx	xxxxx	12	1750	2	1250	14	3000
12. TOTAL		5918		5870		9722		3980		25490
13. Deferred gifts included above[c]					14	2750	3	1350	17	4100

[a] Include all new outright gifts, pledges, deferred gifts, and documented bequest intentions secured during the year. Do not include payments on prior-period pledges or previously deferred gifts or bequests maturing during the year.

[b] Except corporate matching gifts, which should be included in line 9.

[c] Including testamentary commitments.

Expenditures by Category of Expense. A first useful analysis is to look at what development funds are spent on. Most institutional accounting systems can produce a breakdown something like Table 2. The intent of this analysis is to reflect total expenditures on fund raising. Consequently, if you have an independent organization (for example, a separately incorporated alumni association) that does some portion of the fund raising for you, include their costs if you are going to include their proceeds or fund-raising progress. If you have a central development organization and also have personnel and expenses in individual schools or colleges, you will want to include all those costs, but may want to add a "central" and a "decentralized" column to the table shown above to indicate where those costs are incurred.

It will be useful to trace those costs over time at your own institution and to compare them to the costs at other schools. You will probably want to relate these costs to total institutional expenditures as well, calculating development costs as a percentage of E&G (educational and general expenditures), or of total expenditures and transfers. This will be a measure of the extent of the effort the college or university is putting into development.

It is worth pointing out here that institutions do not always expend all development costs on a current basis. In the heavy-investment periods at the start of a campaign, schools will sometimes defer a portion of the costs to be expended in subsequent years against operating budgets or against unrestricted gifts. There are other strategies as well. The point that is relevant here is that you should be sure that your analysis of expenditures includes all expenditures being incurred, regardless of how the institution is handling them.

Expenditures and Staffing by Purpose. The next analysis looks at the various development division activities, and assigns personnel and expenditures to them.

Here you have a choice. The intent of the expenditures-by-category display was to capture all fund-raising-related costs. The intent of the analysis by purpose is to build a cost base with a similar structure to the fund-raising progress base, so that productivity can be assessed. You may wish to try to allocate all costs to specific functions. It may be both simpler and more informative, however, to allocate only personnel costs, on the theory that equipment costs and expenses like travel and telephones and printing support all development activities, and that their allocation is more arbitrary than helpful. You can use the ratio of salaries and wages to total expenditures calculated in Table 2 to distribute support costs to these functions.

Table 3 shows one way of categorizing those activities, and suggests counting personnel and compensation in three groups: exempt, non-exempt, and students. Be sure to include the staffing and personnel costs

Table 2. Development Expenditures by Category (in $Thousands) Sample University, FY 19XX

Payments to development employees:	
Salaries and wages	1,867
Fringe benefits	363
Subtotal	2,230
Payments to non-employees for services	150
Equipment purchase, lease, maintenance[a]	120
Other expenses:	
Travel and entertainment	250
Communications (printing costs, mail, and so on)	300
Telephone, telegraph, and so on	170
Data-processing in your own budget	70
Supplies and other	425
Subtotal	1,215
Total, development division expenditures	3,715
Estimated allocatable data-processing costs	0
Grand total	3,715
Salaries and wages as percent of grand total[b]	50.2

[a] If the equipment is capital, include only the amortization, partial payment, or debt service attributable to the year studied.
[b] Divide the total salaries and wages by grand total expenditures.

of any outside organizations involved in your fund raising, including consultants. The grouping of functions is important. Given differences in the ways development divisions are organized, the subtotals may be more useful than the precise categories.

Again, you will want to track your own institution's records in this format over time, to note the changes and trends. Data in this format also present a good opportunity for comparison with other institutions.

Calculate the ratios of direct fund-raising salaries to total fund-raising expenditures as a rough measure of the share of the division's effort that goes for actual fund raising, as opposed to supporting costs and personnel. Compare institutions on that basis. For a finer breakdown, compare the ratios of salaries and wages to total fund-raising expenditures to see how the development division is dividing its resources among people and support costs. Then compare the ratios of direct fund-raising personnel and salaries to total personnel and salaries to see how much each institution spends to support its direct fund-raising personnel. Compare allocations of non-exempt to exempt to student personnel in each area and overall.

Table 3. Personnel and Salary Expenditures by Purpose Sample University, FY 19XX

Area	FTE Personnel Non-Exempt	FTE Personnel Exempt	FTE Personnel Student[a]	FTE Personnel Total	Personnel Costs ($ in thousands) Non-Exempt	Personnel Costs Exempt	Personnel Costs Student[a]	Personnel Costs Total
Direct fund-raising activities:								
Annual fund	3	3	10	16	52	90	130	272
Major gifts	2	4	—	6	36	160	—	96
Corporations	—	1	—	1	—	45	—	45
Foundations	1	1	—	2	18	40	—	58
Deferred gifts[b]	1	1	—	2	18	50	—	68
School-based programs	10	10	—	220	160	350	—	510
Other	—	—	—	—	—	—	—	—
Subtotal	17	20	10	47	284	735	130	1149
Administration/management activities:								
Administration	4	3	—	7	65	180	—	245
Other	—	—	—	—	—	—	—	—
Subtotal	4	3	—	7	65	180	—	245
Support activities:								
Prospect research	6	1	—	7	105	35	—	140
Gift accounting, DP, donor relations, and so on[c]	13	4	—	17	208	120	—	328
Other	—	—	—	—	—	—	—	—
Subtotal	19	5	—	24	313	155	—	468
Total:	40	28	10	78	662	1070	130	1862
Direct fund-raising salaries as percent of total salaries			61.7					

[a] Consider that 35 hours of student labor equals one FTE.
[b] Deferred giving, planned giving, and so on.
[c] Gift accounting, recording, donor relations, acknowledgements, stewardship, communications with donors, data processing, alumni records, biographical records, and so on. Include only personnel and personnel costs in the development division; do not include personnel in computer centers or elsewhere doing work for the department.

Note that these figures permit you to calculate average compensation for exempt and non-exempt personnel, for the division as a whole, and for personnel in particular functions. You may also wish to compare salary ranges for key personnel. Check the availability and usefulness of data in the annual *Administrative Compensation Surveys* of the College and University Personnel Association before engaging in your own survey.

Productivity: Fund-Raising Progress Versus Expenses

If you have gathered the information called for in the last two sections, you are now in a position to compare fund-raising progress with the associated expenditures.

The most effective single productivity indicator is dollars expended per dollar raised. As shown in Table 4, Sample University raised $25,490,000 and spent $3,710,000 doing it, or 14.6 cents per dollar raised. (See Chapter Two for actual ratios from studies of different institutions.)

Each fund-raising area can be similarly examined. Sample University raised $4,425,000 in annual fund contributions. The direct salaries in this area were $527,000, so the ratio of dollars raised per direct salary was 11.9 cents per dollar. Remember, however, that there are many other people to be paid in the development office besides the direct fund raisers, and there are many other expenses besides salaries. One can construct a "fully loaded" expense for each area by dividing its direct salaries by the ratio of direct salaries to total expenditures. Using the example in Table 4 Sample University's fully loaded costs for annual fund raising were $1,702,000, this results in an expenditure of 38.5 cents per annual fund dollar raised.

This method for allocating costs is obviously only one of many possible approaches; again, it is a vigorous approach rather than a rigorous one. If you have the analytical resources, a preferable approach is to do a detailed allocation of each activity.

In interpreting this productivity analysis, you should keep your institution's history and trajectory in mind. Institutions just starting serious fund raising will be spending more heavily per dollar raised than those with mature programs. Institutions just starting capital campaigns may be investing substantial amounts in prospect evaluation and case statements, long before returns are realized. Finally, consider the converse; institutions that have just completed capital campaigns and have cut back personnel may still reap the benefits of prior solicitations.

Care should be taken in allocating personnel based on these productivity ratios. It is not necessarily true that adding personnel to a highly productive area will produce incremental results at the same time. And you will want to understand and support the overall integrity of the development operation. Annual fund raising, for instance, may have a very high cost per dollar raised, but it may be one of the few links many alumni

Table 4. Fund-Raising Productivity Sample University, FY 19XX

Category	Fund-Raising Progress	Direct Salaries Expenditure	$ exp. divided by $ raised	Total Costs Expenditure[c]	$ exp. divided by $ raised
	($ in thousands)	($ in thousands)	($)	($ in thousands)	($)
Overall	25,490	1,149	0.045	3,710	0.146
By Area:					
Annual fund	4,425[a]	527[b]	0.119	1,702	0.385
Corporations	5,918	45	0.008	145	0.025
Foundations	5,870	58	0.010	187	0.032
Deferred gifts	4,100	68	0.017	220	0.054
Major gifts	5,177[d]	451[e]	0.087	1,456	0.281

Key ratios:
Direct fund-raising salaries as percent of total expenditures: 30.97
Direct fund-raising salaries as percent of total salaries: 61.71
Total salaries as of total expenditures: 50.19

[a] Alumni and non-alumni gifts under $5000 plus corporate matching gifts.
[b] Annual fund expenditures plus one-half of school-based programs.
[c] Direct fund-raising salaries divided by ratio of direct fund-raising salaries to total expenditures.
[d] Alumni and non-alumni gifts of $5000 or more, less deferred gifts.
[e] Major gifts expenditures plus one-half of school-based programs.

have with the institution, and it may serve to identify future major prospects. The productivity ratios can help in allocation decisions, when taken together with prospect analyses and clearly stated missions.

Other Productivity Analyses

While cost per dollar raised is a useful index of fund-raising effectiveness, it does not tell the analyst much about the operations of the division. Except in small institutions, fund-raising activity is susceptible to activity measurement in each area. For each direct fund raiser, one should examine the current number of prospects being followed; the number of cultivation contacts per month; the number of solicitations and amount solicited; the number of gifts and amount given; and the ratios between numbers of solicitations and gifts, and between amounts asked for and given. In other areas, the procedure is analogous: for researchers, how many reports per month?; for "back-room" staff, how many acknowledgments and updates?; and so forth. These indicators can and should be used to plan fund-raising staffing, and can also be used in institutional comparisons.

Environmental and Organizational Questions

You may wish to ask a multitude of questions about the way the fund-raising efforts at your own and other organizations are conducted. The answers to these questions may have some bearing on your costs and productivity. Among these are the following:
- Degree of centralization (for example, all central, development offices in each of the professional schools).
- Relationships with other major organizations that are responsible for fund raising (for example, Is there a separately incorporated alumni organization that solicits funds? How is it related to your office? Annual funds only, or capital?)
- Annual giving programs (for example, Do you run an annual giving program yourself or is it run for you by another organization? Does the other organization direct the use of the funds, for instance to student aid? Do you ask in the annual program only for unrestricted gifts? During a capital campaign do you continue the annual program? With double asks or separating out capital prospects?)
- Alumni composition by program (for example, Do you have a medical school or other units where graduates should be doing better than average? Do you have a high proportion of alumni from graduate arts and sciences programs, now mainly teaching, so potential is low?)

- Relationship with other campaigns (for example, If you have a hospital and medical school, are they campaigning together, or separately?)
- Relationships with organizations not responsible for fund raising but that do contribute funds (for example, Is there a separately incorporated athletic programs club, which contributes funds? Is it part of the overall alumni organization? Are its contributions restricted?)
- Use of volunteers (for example, Advisory only? Major alumni gift solicitation? Used for annual fund only? For reunion giving? Made up of students? Alumni? Others?)
- Use of paid student callers (for example, How extensive in terms of number of calls made? Used only on annual fund?)
- Use of paid outside callers (for example, How extensive in terms of number of calls made? Used only on annual fund?)
- Campaign status (for example, gearing up; in a campaign; phasing out; between campaigns; running series of mini-campaigns; have outgrown the concept and are in campaign mode all the time)
- Growth rate (for example, What is the annual rate of growth that you are planning to try to achieve in fund-raising progress (gifts and pledges) over the next five years?)
- Prospect pool (for example, What is the number of researched prospects you have in each giving category? How is that growing or shrinking over time?)
- Corporate grants and contracts sponsoring research or other direct output (for example, How are such grants handled in your record keeping? Do you handle them through the development office or through a grants and contracts office? How active is your institution in this area?)

You will need to consider, in a more general sense, how the private fund-raising activity on which this chapter is focused relates to overall institutional development activity. This may be the only activity of the development division. Or it may be part of an overall development strategy that includes expansion of service arrangements, federal and state grantsmanship, corporate-university entrepreneurial relationships, and the like. The setting will clearly have much to say about how you wish to be organized, and how private fund-raising fits with the rest of the picture.

Summary

Our main points are simple. Begin at home by collecting the data you would need in any case for the effective management of the development activity. Track the giving patterns over time. Find an appropriate way of categorizing fund-raising expenditures so that they can be linked to the revenues produced by those efforts; calculate the productivity of those efforts. Track changes in these patterns over time as your fund-raising strategy and activity levels change. If possible, follow a pattern in these analyses which your peer institutions can accept, so that you can compare results.

We echo Paton's call in Chapter Two for the "identification of *practical* methods for monitoring development expenditures routinely." We offer the pattern described in this chapter in the hopes that it will contribute to that effort.

John A. Dunn, Jr., Dawn Geronimo Terkla, and Audrey Adam are all in the Institutional Planning Office at Tufts University, as vice-president for planning, director of analytic studies, and researcher/analyst, respectively. As part of the planning and monitoring of Tufts's development efforts, they are currently engaged in a multi-institutional comparative study along the lines set out in this chapter.

Competition for funds from the private sector is intense. Measurement and evaluation of effectiveness in reaching constituencies is essential to success.

Measuring and Expanding Sources of Private Funding

Bruce A. Loessin, Margaret A. Duronio, Georgina L. Borton

Fund raising as a field has experienced rapid growth in recent years and has in common with other growing fields two characteristics: It is a service enterprise and it is increasingly dependent upon complex technology. The growth of fund raising is evident; fund raisers are now at work in most nonprofit sectors of American life, soliciting philanthropic support for museums and zoos, opera companies and symphonies, hospitals and humane societies, and the Statue of Liberty. While fund raising provides a support service for its host institution, the work is actually production- and market-oriented, and clearly entrepreneurial in nature, since success is measured in terms of dollars generated. The technology for planning and accomplishing the work of fund raising has kept pace with its growth in size and importance.

Financing of higher education through fund raising has long been a tradition in American colleges and universities. The importance of fund raising efforts has increased in higher education as the concurrent decline in enrollments, federal revenues, and state support has created actual or potential financial difficulties for many colleges and universities. President Reagan's admonition to the private sector to help replace revenue lost from decreased public support has given fund raisers an added impetus

J. A. Dunn (ed.). *Enhancing the Management of Fund Raising.*
New Directions for Institutional Research, no. 51. San Francisco: Jossey-Bass, Fall 1986.

and confidence. For years development officers requested additional budget allocations for new programs (such as to solicit parents, for regional alumni activities, and for planned giving campaigns), and found the response lukewarm. The importance of these activities was only marginally understood, and it was thought to be unwise in many institutions to invest more dollars in non-academic activities, especially those involving the traditionally misunderstood public relations area. More recently, resource allocations at many institutions have increased significantly for development and the communications operations supporting fund raising. Not only do administrators and trustees better understand the importance of these activities to the survival of the institution, but all concerned are aware that intense competition for funds is now a central factor in this once "gentlemanly" art.

However, the importance of fund raising and the increase in allocations have made it essential that development officers are accountable— for the resources they use, and the results they achieve. Therefore, along with major challenges to solidify the institution's primary, traditional constituencies, and to discover and win support from new constituencies, development officers are under increased pressure to develop or refine data-driven and cost-effective fund-raising methods for both categories of donors.

Measuring Effectiveness in Researching Constituencies

Systematic, formal measurement and evaluation of fund-raising activities is essential to ongoing success. Recent fund-raising literature includes the call from several authors (Blakely, 1985; Rowland, 1985; Willmer, 1985) for more formal evaluation of operating programs. As Rowland stated, "The day of the seat-of-the-pants practitioner is over. Intuition and experience just aren't enough" (1985, p. 8) to ensure successful fund-raising results.

Measuring effectiveness means to answer the question: "Do these efforts produce the desired results?" As indicated in other sections of this volume, measuring effectiveness requires more than a simple review of bottom-line figures, more than a general comparison of this year's achievements with last year's, and more than a quick assessment of an individual institution's performance with its peers. Evaluation must be as sophisticated as the fund-raising process itself. Results and efforts must be carefully assessed, along with factors affecting results and efforts.

There is general agreement in the literature (see, for instance, Beyer, 1975; Kotler, 1982; Smith, 1981) that the results of a fund-raising program are best measured and evaluated against the goals for the program. As Kotler indicated, there are three possible approaches to goal setting. The first is the incremental approach, in which a goal figure is derived from an analysis of last year's revenues, this year's inflation rate, and estimates of other economic conditions. The second is the needs approach, in which the goal figure is based on forecasted needs. The third approach, that recommended by Kotler, is the opportunity approach, in which goal setting begins with the question: How much money could be raised from each donor group with different levels of fund-raising expenditures?

Part of the answer to this question could be found by applying Pickett's (1982) method for determining an institution's potential for voluntary support. This method identifies the amount of money available in the institution's environment and the institution's access to these resources. The amount of available money can be determined through examination of such variables as number of alumni, number of families with annual income over a certain level in the geographical area, and total value of grants made by major foundations in the institution's state. Access to resources can be determined through examination of such variables as enrollment, cost of attendance, and value of endowment. When potential for voluntary support has been assessed in this way, the results can be used to set appropriate goals and to measure success in development efforts. Determining goals using the opportunity approach allows for the identification of new sources and new strategies for solicitation for both traditional and new sources and for the examination of relationships between solicitation costs and expected results.

Measuring effectiveness in reaching constituencies depends upon thorough data-based knowledge of four elements in fund raising. These elements are (1) the market (the total pool of actual and potential donors), (2) fund-raising processes, (3) the environment, and (4) actual results or outcomes. It is important to note that, while narrative descriptions and anecdotal information are valuable in evaluation, as are experience and intuition, measurement implies the use of hard data—that is, numbers— to substantiate judgments and inform decisions.

Measurement that results in useful information requires:
- precise definitions of the variables to be measured
- documentation (numbers, kinds, and descriptions) of activities, results, and events
- survey research to generate data not readily available or to create new data
- appropriate management information systems for data gathering, storage, access, and analysis
- quantification of hard-to-quantify aspects of fund raising, such as methods, donor attitudes, and market characteristics
- pre-established standards (such as historical or comparative norms) against which to compare measures.

While development officers must assume responsibility for deciding which questions to ask and which variables are most important to measure, institutional researchers can be most helpful in devising measurement and quantification systems, instruments, and methods for identifying standards and for collecting and analyzing data. Researchers can also assist development officers in interpreting data to illuminate trends and patterns in donor characteristics; to determine differences among groups of donors; and to identify significant relationships among methods, groups, and results.

Planning for Effectiveness

Measurement systems not only provide critical information to assess progress but also provide the basis for planning. Fund-raising goals, the essential criteria for evaluating success, cannot be sound without competent planning. Arguments for planning include the following:

Planning enhances the taking of initiative in a field in which initiative has never been more critical. A conscientious, rational planning process is a systematic method for generating new ideas as well as for scrutinizing current practices and perspectives. Without a formal planning process, the temptation can be overwhelming to proceed on some present, but not fully effective, course, only because "we have always done it this way."

Planning provides structure and support for major activities in a field where crises, restraints, and occasionally, new options, are likely to occur. In some cases unplanned events can yield funds, but in most cases they do not. Commitment to a well-developed plan helps to ensure that attention, time, and resources will be devoted to the right activities.

Planning helps to achieve a goal orientation and to identify the best use of executive and staff time. Increasingly, development officers are facing production expectations more similar to those faced by business executives than by academic administrators in other areas of the institution. Planning provides previously established schedules and time-tables against which progress can be measured.

Planning illuminates the need to develop priorities and to differentiate among potential donors and various methods. Development officers and staff cannot do everything and see everyone. Planning helps to target those donors and methods offering the most potential for new dollars.

Planning fosters a long-term view and provides support for activities not expected to have an immediate payoff. Successful solicitation of new donors in many cases involves a lengthy process of identifying and cultivating new markets. A commitment to allocate resources for long-term efforts can only result from planning.

Planning in the production-oriented field of fund raising is to provide the map and impetus for action and must always be understood as the means to an end. Although planners in development must maintain a goal orientation, they must also have a process orientation that allows for adjustment to ever-changing environmental conditions. The shelf-life of plans for development is limited because fund-raising results are easily affected by changes on the institutional level, as well as at the regional, state, and national levels. Factors that may affect the institution's relationship with major changes of donors can be altered practically overnight by such events as a stir among area ethnic groups; strikes, work stoppages, and plant closing; a winning (or losing) football team; or the retirement of a popular college president. Development plans should always be flexible enough to allow for conforming, either temporarily or permanently, with the latest changes in constituency environments and behaviors.

Reaching Traditional Constituencies

Economy and effectiveness in fund raising depend on a loyal and dependable funding base so that educational organizations can count on a certain amount of money each year. If an institution were to re-create every donor every year, operating costs would be prohibitive. In higher education institutions, alumni and local corporations and foundations have provided the dependable funding base.

Alumni make up the core of traditional donors. It is well understood that alumni interest and involvement are as vital to overall success as are the actual dollars they provide (Forman, 1984). The involvement of alumni in actual fund-raising projects and activities results in an affirmed psychological commitment to the institution and generates enthusiasm and momentum for reaching those who are less committed. The other vital traditional constituency upon which most institutions depend includes regional businesses and foundations. These local organizations usually accept the logic of providing philanthropic support to higher education institutions in their own communities. The human resources needed by local corporations are often provided by neigboring educational institutions. The success of the local university can have far-reaching effects on the overall economy of an area. For example, in Pittsburgh the enormous combined resources of two of America's major research universities (University of Pittsburgh and Carnegie-Mellon University) are significantly helping to revitalize the economy of western Pennsylvania.

Alumni and local corporations and foundations have until recently provided relatively stable primary markets for individual institutions. Although most institutions find it unnecessary to re-create each donor each year, traditional sources of support can no longer be taken for granted. Efforts by competing fund seekers, either from other educational institutions or other kinds of organizations, threaten to "raid" and debilitate a given institution's traditional funding base. Competition for vital resources in higher education—not only for funds, but also for students and key faculty and administrators—is at an unprecedented high, as is competition among all non-profit organizations. College and university administrators now realize that their institutions share a common concern with business corporations—the possibility of erosion of their primary markets. Resources must be allocated to strengthen and solidify the base of traditional donors, as well as to measure effectiveness with these donors.

Measuring effectiveness in reaching traditional donors is increasingly important, since it is the only way to determine if this fundamental base of support is shrinking. Various indexes might be employed, such as percentage of alumni giving, mean or median gift size, and the ratio of total dollars received to operating budget. These measures can be compared with the institution's own past history and with these or similar measures from peer institutions.

The most recent report (1986) on voluntary support to education prepared by the Council for Financial Aid to Education (CFAE) contains substantial information about fund-raising outcomes that provides national standards against which to measure institutional performance. For instance, the survey reports number of individual gifts and total amounts by type of institution. Medians of these totals can be used as norms against which to measure institutional performance in individual gifts.

With increased operating demands, development officers often will not have the time, and may not have the expertise, to fully use the information provided by CFAE. Institutional researchers could make an important contribution to fund-raising processes by helping development officers identify and use to advantage more of the available information than is probably being used in the typical fund-raising operation.

The Challenge of the Nontraditional Donor

In addition to maintaining the support of traditional donors, most higher education institutions in the last decade have been interested in finding new donors and ways to cultivate them. However, institutions vary considerably in the manner in which fund raising is undertaken and whether sources outside traditional constituencies are solicited. Advancement programs with a national scope, or those designed to reach nontraditional donors, are underway for perhaps only a few of America's colleges and universities.

Practical experience demonstrates that the fundamental necessity for developing support among less traditional donors is the enlargement and solidification of the traditional funding base. It is rare for an institution to be successful with less easily reached constituents if charity has not begun at home. The expertise, sophistication, and scope of contacts necessary for reaching nontraditional sources can usually only be acquired through learning how to be successful on more modest local levels. Furthermore, nationally oriented donors will ask questions regarding traditional sources of funding and will carefully evaluate the answers. Increasing numbers and amounts of gifts from traditional donors create sign posts that nontraditional evaluators will use to determine the appropriateness of their support and of certain levels of giving.

Nevertheless, success at home does not automatically ensure success with a larger market because philosophies, methods, schedules, and budget formulas must be altered when cultivating the nontraditional donor. The philosophy underlying appeals to alumni is based on nostalgia and, to local corporations, on a mutually beneficial relationship. Appeals to donors outside the traditional category must usually be preceded by efforts to convince donors that they also have a relationship to the institution. These appeals should most often emphasize what the institution is currently accomplishing. More preliminary work is necessary to increase nontraditional donors' awareness and appreciation of the institution. These preliminary activities usually require a longer time before returns on investment occur. Similarly, overall efforts to reach nontraditional donors may initially cost more, per dollar raised, than efforts to maintain support of traditional donors. This fact must be considered when new efforts are planned. Although individual institutions will find it impractical to explore every new potential constituency, creative thinkers at each kind and size of institution will be able to identify new possibilities that are appropriate to that institution's history, goals, and budget considerations.

Nontraditional donors may be found among several existing institutional constituencies or may require the development of new constituencies, as will be discussed below. Measuring effectiveness with these donors can be accomplished by using many of the same indexes indicated for traditional donors. It may also be that institutional researchers can suggest other possibilities for measuring effectiveness that take into account the special techniques, efforts, and skills necessary for successful solicitation of these donors.

Nontraditional Donors: Individuals

Nontraditional individual donors may fit into one of the following classifications:

Secondary Affiliation. Parents of students are examples of potential donors in this group. Faculty and staff might also be included at some institutions. These potential donors have a more logical reason for supporting a given institution than the man on the street, but colleges often overlook or under-use their relationships with these donors. Many institutions do not have systematic mechanism for fund-raising activities with members of this group.

For instance, as reported by CFAE (1985), 718 institutions (64 percent) reported contributions from parents, totaling, $54,809,000, or 5 percent of the total non-alumni individual contribution. The majority of institutions (83 percent) reporting parent contributions were private; these institutions raised 94 percent of the total in this category. Nevertheless, 124 public institutions raised $3,372,000 from parents. Perhaps the important fact to note about these data is not how few public institutions reported contributions from parents, but that 156 private institutions did not report contributions from parents. If, in fact, this means that parents were not solicited at these institutions, this represents a sizable loss.

The average total gift per institution from parents was $86,594. Multiplying this number by the number of private institutions not reporting income from this source amounts to $13,508,664 in lost opportunity. This amount represents an average 21 percent increase in the overall total from non-alumni individuals. Although speculative, these data suggest an estimate of the potential gains from effective solicitation of new sources.

"Users." Many educational institutions also overlook the numbers of people who come into contact with the institution but who are not students, alumni, or faculty and staff. These are members of the community who are exposed to and often attend the school's noncredit learning activities, athletic, cultural, and entertainment events, and those who take advantage of services available to the general community. Vendors who supply the institution with services and products may also fall into this group. Names and addresses of these potential donors, along with general information about their interests, are easily obtainable from institutional records not ordinarily used for development purposes. Even if contact between the institution and these potential donors is marginal, the institution may have a slight advantage over other competitors for funds.

Institutional researchers could be invaluable to the development officer in helping to devise strategies to estimate potential numbers of donors and total revenues from this source. For instance, a brief survey of a random sample of these constituents that asks questions about income range, interest level, and willingness to donate, could generate the data needed to use the chain ratio method (Kotler, 1982) to analyze the giving potential of this donor pool. This method involves multiplying a base number by a succession of percentages to lead to a defined donor set. Using surveyed enrollees of the institution's informal programs as an example, the following formula results:

> Total number of enrollees (base number) times the percent who are financially able to give times the percent who have high interest in the institution times the percent who are willing to donate equals the estimate of market potential.

Therefore, if an institution has 2000 enrollees each year, of whom 65 percent are judged to be able to give, of whom 72 percent are interested in the institution, and of whom 20 percent are willing to donate, 187 donors (2000 × .65 × .72 × .20) can be predicted from this pool. The development officer now has a forecast of potential upon which to base campaign decisions for solicitations of this group.

Regionally Based "Friends." There are many individuals in the institution's geographical area who did not graduate from the institution, and whose children did not attend the institution, but who nevertheless may be amenable to an approach for funds and who will give if they can be convinced that they have something to gain by giving. Several approaches may be used. The most obvious is to appeal to community interest, pride, and loyalty. Funding requests that emphasize the importance of the educational and cultural wealth of the community can be successful with these potential donors. One purpose of the higher education institution is to preserve and transmit the culture of a community; this mission may not always be clear to community members. Therefore, fund raisers can increase chances for success by preceding solicitation with public relations activities that emphasize the institution's importance to the community.

Another approach is to emphasize the shared interest of non-affiliated donors and special programs or services of the institution. For instance, members of the local chamber music society may be convinced to support music programs at the university. A third approach is to appeal to the individual's desire to increase personal prestige through association with the institution. As is the case with alumni, new donors from any of the above groups have value to the institution beyond the actual money they might contribute. Persons from these groups may never have been personally invited by a respected institution to contribute their time and services, and may welcome the opportunity to join other volunteers, whose contribution to fund-raising success has long been understood.

Information about the identity of individual donors or of groups of donors is usually best obtained through the personal contacts and word-of-mouth activities of development and other institutional representatives. Because of this, the development office staff may need to formally educate and encourage other members of the institutional community, most notably the faculty, about the significant role they can play in helping the institution to develop new friendships. Lunchtime seminars, for instance, during which a skilled development professional suggests how faculty can be effective in informally promoting new relationships for the university might be helpful. Several major organizations now have incentive programs to encourage employees to help recruit new staff for key or hard-to-fill positions. Why not programs within institutions of higher education to provide appropriate recognition and appreciation to employees who help the institution to cultivate new donors?

Nontraditional Donors: Corporations and Foundations Outside the Geographical Region

For most higher education institutions, there is no more difficult fund-raising task than that of securing funds from major corporations and foundations with which the institution has had no historical connection. The importance of success with traditional donors as a basis for approaching these nontraditional donors cannot be overemphasized. Efforts will most likely fail if support from Fortune 500 corporations and major foundations is sought without evidence of considerable success with natural constituencies. However, realistic efforts in the solicitation of new corporate and foundation donors can be profitable, as some colleges and universities have demonstrated. Breaking through regional barriers, even if only in one instance, not only gains support for the institution from that one new donor, but also creates a nationwide arena of potential givers. Just as nationally oriented donors will be interested in successful fund raising among traditional sources, they are also likely to be favorably impressed if the institution has established a support base among other nontraditional donors. Practical experience, supported by the results of a study by the Taft Corporation ("Reslicing a Shrinking Pie," 1985) indicates that the most suitable approach for institutions seeking to break through regional boundaries is to concentrate on programmatic ties between the institution and the specific corporation or foundation. Demonstration of a shared concern or important common goal can set the stage for a hearing and begin the process of making geographically distant corporation and foundation officials aware of the institution's strengths, accomplishments, and aspirations.

This suggests the need for diligent research by the institution to identify major corporations and foundations that have both the financial ability to give and a commonality of philosophy, interests, and goals. Hall (1984) suggested a five-step program to follow in seeking support from a major foundation. The steps she suggested are summarized as follows: (1) preparation of the institution's statement of needs and priorities; (2) identification of foundations whose interests "truly overlap" (p. 20) with the institution's stated needs; (3) cultivation of a specific program officer at the foundation; (4) solicitation through a formal proposal that meets the specifications of the foundation; and (5) stewardship after receipt of the grant, not only to keep foundation leaders informed, but also to lay the groundwork for a later proposal. Success with this group of nontraditional donors often involves a long and sometimes delicate process, requiring persistence, patience, and the ability to weather temporary setbacks. Nevertheless, effective research and planning, supported by successful efforts with traditional donors, can greatly increase the odds of success.

Forms of Giving

The most traditional form of giving is the donation of cash, either directly or indirectly (in the form of royalties or annuities). Occurring less frequently, but also in the traditional category, are noncash donations that may include items such as real estate and private collections of books, art, and other objects. Occasionally, an institution will receive a business to run or to sell. Institutional administrators are usually aware that this type of gift entails responsibility and possible cash investments that must be considered when determining the actual value of the gift. According to CFAE (1986), corporations are increasing their gifts of company products and property, particularly data-processing and research equipment. Gifts in this form accounted for 18.8 percent of total corporate giving in 1984–1985.

Reaching New Donors

As most institutions become more dependent on the private sector and are more market-oriented, new methods for raising money from both new and traditional constituencies are emerging nationwide. These activities involve procedures that are either entirely new to many institutions or have become so sophisticated at larger institutions that they hardly resemble earlier versions of the same general method.

Phone-othons and Phone/Mail Programs. That fund raising is more and more supported by high technology is indicated by the use of complex, sophisticated, and extensive mechanisms for phone and mail solicitations. Firms that specialize in creating phone/mail systems are operating successfully throughout the country. Persons reached by these methods may be "never givers" in the alumni pool. They may also be part of other constituencies, such as people who attend major college events or who live in neighborhoods that immediately surround the college.

It should be noted that phone and mail campaign efforts, as well as outcomes, can be measured and evaluated in direct ways, enabling development executives to establish clear performance standards and individual goals with development staff (including paid students). After baseline data are accumulated, standards for numbers of calls completed, pledges obtained, and for pledges increased, for instance, can easily be set. Staff performance evaluation is a critical part of assessing and understanding the overall effectiveness of any development effort. This type of evaluation is often considered to be an activity important only to the human resources staff or to the staff member personally. Its importance to final fund-raising results is often overlooked.

Marketing and Management Information Systems. Most early alumni and development data systems, even at institutions with the highest rates of philanthropic support, were essentially developed from alumni listing and gift recording systems. There was no mechanism for prospecting clients. In the last five years there has been a surge of new information systems, particularly at major research and prestigious private institutions. Systems can be designed to provide information for identifying, cultivating, and soliciting new donors who are far outside the realms of alumni and hometown businesses. Some major university development offices have their own significantly-sized computer hardware, custom-built marketing software, and a staff of computer experts to maximize opportunities for discovering new prospects.

However, concerns have been raised regarding increased sophistication in the technology of fund raising. Pray (1981), for instance, noted that since at many institutions large shares of the totals received for voluntary support come from a few people, time and money spent being "efficient" with computers may divert personal attention from the "very significant 50 or 100 people," and recommended that development officers cultivate "insight into the principle of emphasis where it counts" (p. 386). Elsewhere in this volume, Paton describes a possible situation in which traditional donors have reached their limits of predisposition (willingness to give) and capacity (ability to give). If this is the case, following Pray's recommendation to put emphasis where it counts could mean using new technologies to identify new sources.

As mentioned earlier, constituency market research is a tool for estimating and predicting those situations where enhanced efforts or completely new efforts may count a great deal. Although no overall information exists to describe current procedures in higher education institutions, Willmer (1985) found that only 26 percent of small colleges conducted market analyses of donor constituencies. Since common sense and experience demonstrate that not everyone in a given pool, even among alumni, is a potential donor, research leading to informed decision making (research that helps to predict such factors as numbers of new donors, size of gifts, and cost of solicitation efforts) is imperative.

Regionalization and Travel. If traditional givers are close to home, it stands to reason that nontraditional givers are somewhere out "in the field" and that is exactly where key development personnel from many institutions are spending most of their time. A university's alumni, living far from the geographical area of the institution, can provide enormous support and resources to development staff by introducing them to new funding sources that may have been totally unaware of the school's mission, or even existence. Many of the strongest advancement programs have enhanced their chances of securing support from new donors not only by sending staff out in the field but also by organizing their efforts by region, with certain advancement personnel concentrating on certain cities or geographical regions.

New Intra-Institutional Alliances. As indicated earlier, members of the college or university community can be encouraged to help development offices identify new prospects. In the search for new methods for reaching constituencies, chief administrators and development officers in many institutions have discovered the opportunity to encourage new intra-institutional alliances between and among traditionally distant factions, such as non-academic administrators and faculty. Members of both groups have learned that generating critical revenues from new sources requires the combined expertise of development professionals and faculty. In the creation of a sophisticated, complex proposal, development officers might provide the necessary process expertise, while the content expertise is provided by the faculty.

Conclusion

Although it is certain that the competition for funds will continue to exist and even to expand, the good news is that, overall, attempts to retain the commitment of past donors and to develop new sources of revenue can be highly successful. Development officers must use all resources available, including the skills and expertise of others, to reach traditional and new donors, and to develop and test new methods.

References

Beyer, K. G. "How to Organize and Evaluate a Development Program." In *The President's Role in Development.* Washington, D.C.: Association of American Colleges, 1975.
Blakely, B. E. "Mutual Support." *Currents,* 1985, *11* (7), 64.
Council for Financial Aid to Education. *Voluntary Support to Education 1983-1985.* New York: CFAE, 1985.
Council for Financial Aid to Education. *Voluntary Support to Education 1984-1985.* New York: CFAE, 1986.
Forman, R. G. "A-L-U-M-N-I Doesn't Just Spell Money." *CASE Currents,* 1984, *10* (8), 26-29.
Hall, M. R. "Breaking Into the Foundation Big Time." *CASE Currents,* 1984, *10,* 18-22.
Kotler, P. *Marketing for Nonprofit Organizations.* Englewood Cliffs, N.J.: Prentice-Hall, 1982.
Pickett, W. L. "What Determines Fund-Raising Effectiveness?" *Currents,* 1982, *8* (1), 22-25.
Pray, F. C. "New Perspectives on Current Issues." In F. C. Pray (ed.), *Handbook for Educational Fund Raising: A Guide to Successful Principles and Practices for Colleges, Universities, and Schools.* San Francisco: Jossey-Bass, 1981.
"Reslicing a Shrinking Pie." *CASE Currents,* 1985, *11* (7), 20.
Rowland, H. R. "No More Flying Blind." *CASE Currents,* 1985, *11* (7), 7-9.
Smith, D. C. "Appropriate Goals for Giving Programs and Capital Campaigns." In F. C. Pray (ed.), *Handbook for Educational Fund Raising: A Guide to Successful Principles and Practices for Colleges, Universities, and Schools.* San Francisco: Jossey-Bass, 1981.

Williams, W. K. "Beyond Knee-Jerk Thinking." *CASE Currents*, 1984, *10* (1), 72.
Willmer, W. K. "A Large View of Small Colleges." *CASE Currents*, 1985, (7), 18–21.

Bruce A. Loessin is vice-president for development at the University of Pittsburgh.

Margaret A. Duronio is a research associate in the Office of the Vice-President for Development at the University of Pittsburgh.

Georgina L. Borton is director of special projects in the Office of the Vice-President for Development at the University of Pittsburgh.

Graphics, survey research, and multivariate statistical techniques were applied at a private liberal arts college to help development professionals better understand and predict alumni giving behavior, both on an aggregate and individual basis.

Understanding and Predicting Alumni Giving Behavior

Michael S. Connolly, Rene Blanchette

Following the microeconomic model described by Jeffry Paton in Chapter Two, alumni giving behavior is theoretically a function of capacity and motivation. Put simply, whether alumni contribute to their institution depends on their financial ability to do so, and on their willingness to part with their money. Although the model is straightforward, the development professional is faced with a sizable challenge. Since the actual wealth and income of alumni are rarely reported, they must be measured indirectly by accumulating information on professions, job titles, major assets such as houses and boats on which values can be placed, and security holdings as reported in financial statements. The willingness of individual alumni to give is perhaps even more elusive for the development professional. This information also comes from a variety of sources, and over the years the development professional builds up a list of alumni who are friendly to the institution.

Development professionals thus focus most of their attention on individual alumni. This makes good sense, because after all, individual alumni must be solicited for donations. However, this approach is not practical when working with large numbers of alumni. We therefore decided to begin our analysis of alumni giving behavior by looking at aggregations of alumni with an eye toward eventually describing and predicting the giving behavior of individuals.

What follows is a description of what we think has been a very successful beginning at Wesleyan University, a private liberal arts college. We report no new statistical methodologies; rather, we show how we applied three well-known and time-tested techniques: graphics, survey research, and discriminant analysis. By using graphics, we pose basic questions about how demographic factors may influence alumni capacity and motivation at the aggregate level. The survey research provides a host of measures on alumni attitudes that reflect the latent variable, willingness to give. We employ discriminant analysis to combine this information with our demographic data to produce a more detailed (but simplified) description of aggregate giving behavior. Finally, we use the models derived from discriminant analysis to predict the giving behavior of individual alumni. At each stage, we relate our analysis to the university's fund-raising strategy.

Forming the Aggregate Groups

We group Wesleyan's alumni by four demographic categories: (1) class year, (2) sex, (3) geographic region, and (4) career occupation. These categories are actually independent variables that influence alumni giving behavior, for imbedded in each are the variables described above: ability and willingness to give. On the one hand, alumni from earlier classes are probably more able to contribute than those from more recent classes because they are better established in their careers. On the other hand, older alumni may be less willing to give than younger alumni because their interest in the school may have waned over the years. It therefore makes good sense to develop a clear understanding of these fundamental demographic characteristics.

We accomplish this by simply graphing the number of alumni against five-year class intervals (Figure 1, Exhibit 1A), sex from 1974 to 1980 since Wesleyan became coeducational in the early 1970s, (Figure 2, Exhibit 2A), career occupation (Figure 3, Exhibit 3A), and geographic region (Figure 4, Exhibit 4A). Although these graphs reveal nothing surprising, they are quite informative. For example, since 1945 the number of Wesleyan's alumni has steadily grown, leveling off only in the last few years (Figure 1, Exhibit 1A). Ten to fifteen years ago it may have been possible to approach prospect research exclusively at the level of individual alumni; clearly this is not the case today. Figure 2 (Exhibit 2A) shows that the number of female alumni has been gradually growing over the last seven years, resulting in nearly even sex ratios for the Classes of 1977 to 1980. This suggests that fund-raising strategies will have to be adjusted in response to the increasing proportion of females. Figure 3 (Exhibit 3A) reveals that Wesleyan graduates pursue business careers in far greater numbers than any of the other professions. This is even more evident when the alumni who are directors and officers of corporations are combined with those in the general business category. Finally, Figure 4 (Exhibit 4A) clearly shows that many more alumni live in the Eastern and New England states than in other regions of the country.

The Demographics of Alumni Giving Behavior

Having described Wesleyan's alumni demographically, we now ask how these demographic characteristics influence alumni giving behavior. Can we characterize ability and willingness to give by describing the past giving behavior of alumni at these aggregate levels? Can this result in an increased understanding of alumni giving behavior and inform fund-raising strategies?

There are two basic ways to measure alumni giving. The percentage of each demographic group making any contribution, however big or small, can be computed. This measure can be viewed to be a function of alumni loyalty (Dunn and Hutten, 1983). The second way to represent giving is to calculate the median number of dollars contributed by individual alumni in each demographic group (half of the alumni contribute less than the median, half contribute more). This measure is probably related to both alumni loyalty and wealth (Dunn and Hutten, 1983). Since alumni giving behavior may vary from year to year, we used three-year totals in our analysis by simply summing the amount each graduate contributed from 1983 to 1985. The percentage of each group giving and the median gift were based on these three-year totals.

Our measures can thus be related to the microeconomic model of donor giving behavior described by Paton in Chapter Two. That is, loyalty (or willingness to give) is linked to the latent variable motivation, while wealth (or ability) is closely associated with alumni capacity. The problem then is to find ways to measure these variables and determine how they affect the two dimensions of alumni giving behavior: percentage of the group contributing and the size of individual alumni contributions within the groups. Loyalty and motivation are really latent variables, for there is no single measure that best quantifies them. The survey research that we describe in detail below has allowed us to get a handle on this complex question. Wealth, however, can in theory be quantified, but in practice few alumni are willing to provide information about their income and net worth. Indirect measures, such as the demographic characteristic of career occupation, must therefore be developed for this independent variable as well.

Two major strategies can be employed to meet the goals and objectives of a fund-raising campaign: (1) involve young alumni in the campaign, even if the average gift is small; and (2) increase the number of alumni giving in the higher categories (McCaskey and Dunn, 1983; Dunn,

Figure 1. Gifts by Class Year

Figure 1A. Number of Alumni

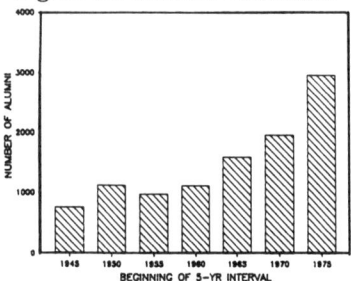

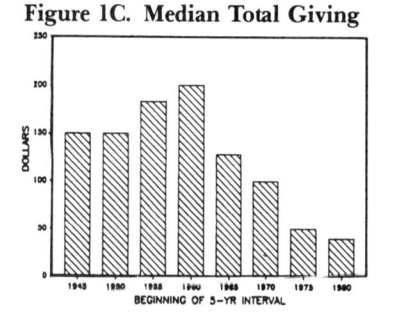

Figure 1B. Participation in Annual Giving

Figure 1C. Median Total Giving

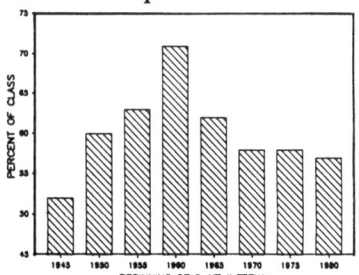

Figure 1D. Gifts > $1000

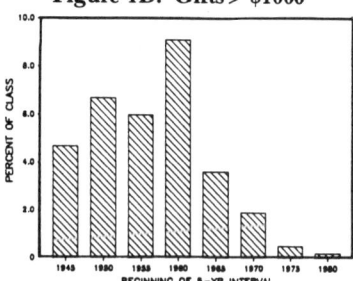

Figure 2. Gifts by Alumni Gender

Figure 2A. Number of Alumni

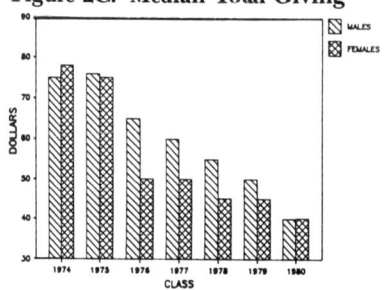

Figure 2B. Participation in Annual Giving

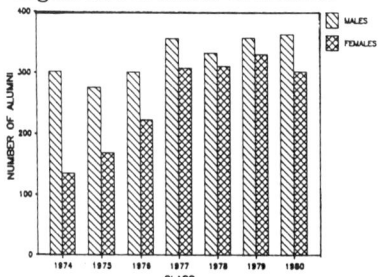

Figure 2C. Median Total Giving

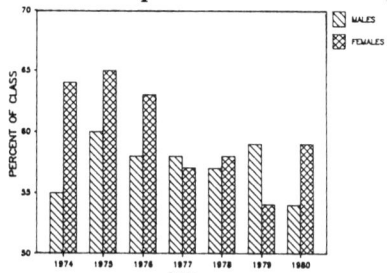

Figure 2D. Gifts > $1000

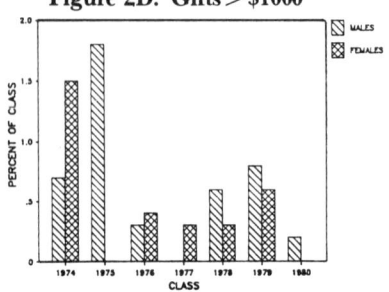

Figure 3. Gifts by Career Occupation

Figure 3A. Number of Alumni

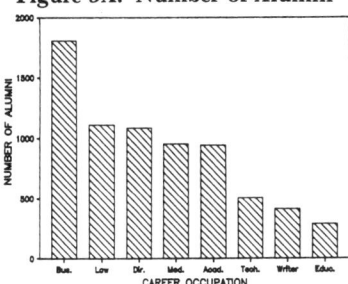

Figure 4B. Participation in Annual Giving

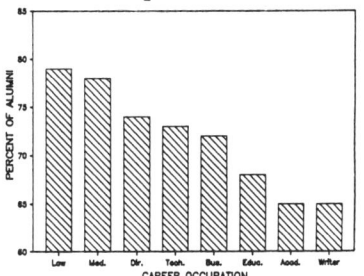

Figure 3C. Median Total Giving

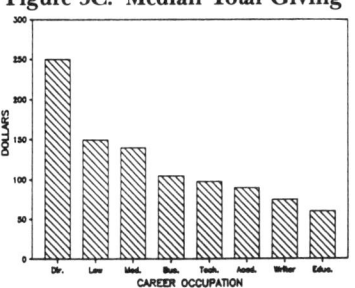

Figure 3D. Gifts > $1000

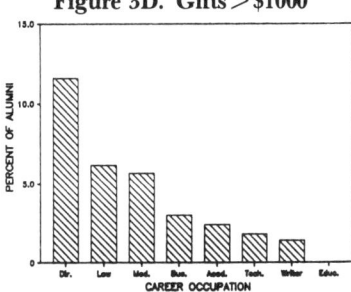

Figure 4. Gifts by Geographic Region

Figure 4A. Number of Alumni

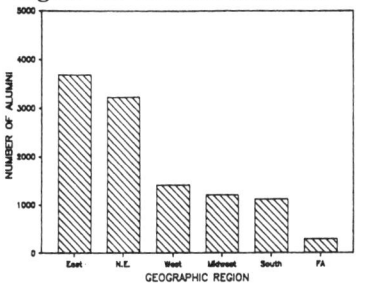

Figure 3B. Participation in Annual Giving

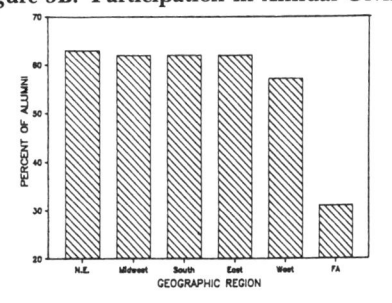

Figure 4C. Median Total Giving

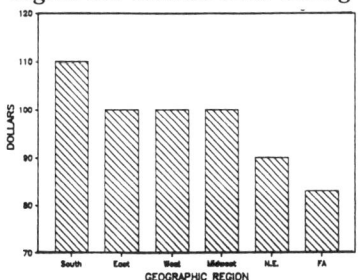

Figure 4D. Gifts > $1000

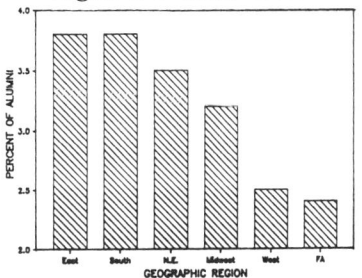

1985). The percentage of alumni giving provides a measure of how well the first strategy is being pursued. Since our primary goal is to tie the analysis to actual fund-raising strategies, we gauge performance with respect to the second strategy by also calculating the percentage of alumni in each demographic group contributing more than one thousand dollars over the three-year period.

Contributions by Class Year. We begin our analysis by focusing on the giving behavior of alumni in different classes. To facilitate the analysis, we grouped alumni at five-year intervals, beginning at 1945 and ending in 1979. By making two assumptions about motivation and capacity, and applying them to the microeconoimc model described earlier, we were able to accurately predict alumni giving behavior across these groups. The two assumptions are as follows:

1. Motivation should decline steadily as alumni grow older because they identify less with the institution than younger alumni.

2. Capacity should increase as alumni develop their careers. Therefore, alumni in earlier classes should be able to give more than more recent graduates.

The second assumption merely states the obvious. In contrast, although appealing in an intuitive sense the first assumption has not been supported by hard data. The class reunion survey conducted in 1985 by the Development Office at Wesleyan has helped fill this void. Specifically, alumni from classes ending in zero or five (that is, the Classes of 1945, 1950, . . . , 1980) were asked a host of questions relating to alumni interest and loyalty. One question specifically asked alumni how they felt about substantially increasing their annual gift. A plot of the percentage of each class responding positively to this question reveals a steady decline in positive responses from the Class of 1980 to the Class of 1945 (Figure 5). We interpret this result as strong support for our first assumption.

What then is our prediction? Our assumptions suggest that capacity and motivation should be operating counter to each other. That is, as alumni giving capacity is on the rise, alumni motivation to part with their wealth is on the decline. We therefore should expect alumni giving to increase over the most recent classes to a plateau, and then decrease to the immediate post-World War II classes. Our prediction should hold for all three measures of alumni giving. Indeed, this is exactly what we see. From 1980 to the class interval 1960–1964 (the Class of 1980 is individually plotted), all three measures of giving increase and then fall off to the 1945–1949 class interval (see Figure 1, Exhibits 1B through 1D).

How can these results inform fund-raising strategy? By combining what we have learned with the demographics of class size (Figure 1, Exhibit 1A), we clearly see that the classes of the last decade present a golden marketing opportunity. Not only are these alumni becoming more able to give at a time they continue to be willing to give, but they are doing so in extremely large numbers. The importance of loyalty in this

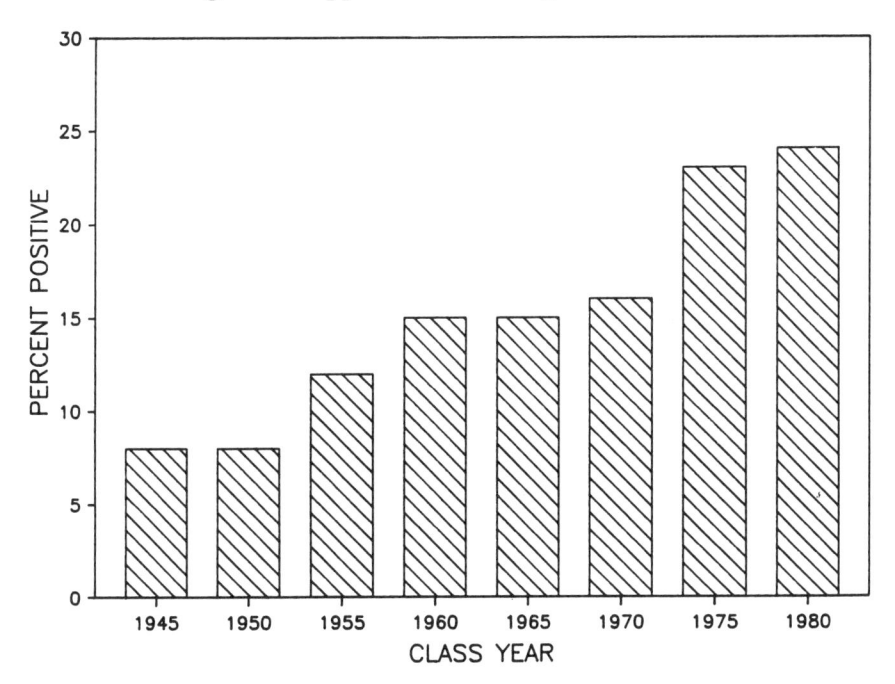

Figure 5. Support for Increasing Annual Gifts

group emerges by noting that the percentage of 1945-1949 alumni giving drops well below the percentage for the most recent classes. Nevertheless, even though the level of giving falls off, older alumni still contribute more on an individual basis than do younger alumni. This suggests that willingness to give indeed may be fleeting and that the time to strike is now. In other words, following the strategy described above, the younger alumni should be actively solicited for contributions, no matter how small their gifts might be. Instead of giving up on these prospects because of the low cost effectiveness of soliciting them, efforts should be made to track and involve them. This heavy investment in alumni loyalty should pay off in the future decades as the giving potential of these individuals matures (Dunn, 1985). Finally, older alumni from the last decade should be asked to steadily increase their gifts, while the best strategy after the plateau is reached might be to cultivate those alumni who continue to contribute, making sure that they know they are appreciated.

Contributions by Sex. Figure 2 (Exhibits 2B through 2D) conveys two types of information. First, since giving behavior is plotted separately for each class from 1974 to 1980, a finer grain analysis is provided for the classes of the last decade. Second, because the data are broken out by sex, they can be examined for differences in female and male giving behavior. As we expected, overall alumni contributions increase from 1980 to 1974;

median total giving exhibits the clearest trend (Figure 2, Exhibit 2C). Not much can be said about the plot for the percentage of alumni making large contributions (Figure 2, Exhibit 2D) because so few of these young alumni make large gifts. In addition, the pattern in this figure is erratic, which suggests that giving at high levels from younger alumni is highly unpredictable. These findings are relevant to the fund-raising strategy described above; young alumni should be encouraged to participate, but not much effort should be expended soliciting them for large gifts.

The separate plots for female and male alumni giving behavior provided us with some surprises with respect to the percentage of alumni giving (Figure 2, Exhibit 2B) and the median total gift (Figure 2, Exhibit 2C). Although the median total gift is the same for both sexes in 1980, the level of giving increases for males at a faster rate over the next four classes. However, females catch up with the males in the Class of 1975 and this equality is maintained in the Class of 1974. Turning toward the percentage of female and male alumni giving in each class, we see that the rate of participation exhibits no clear pattern in the four most recent class years plotted. Somewhat unexpectedly, though, this measure jumps over five percentage points for 1976 females, but not for the males. This difference between the sexes is maintained in the Classes of 1975 and 1974.

Our findings have implications for the formulation of fund-raising tactics in the more recent classes. Specifically, females ten years out are somewhat more loyal to the institution and on the average give just as much as their male counterparts. Folding this interpretation into the demographics of Wesleyan's classes (Figure 2, Exhibit 2A) tels us that we should be planning on paying more attention to females in the most recent classes. Since Wesleyan became coeducational only in the early 1970s, we have no way to tell whether these relationships in giving behavior will continue further down the line. This indeed complicates our fund-raising efforts a bit. We will have to track the contributions of the 1974 and 1975 females and be prepared to modify our tactics if we see changes in their giving behavior. This approach goes to the heart of what strategic planning is all about and speaks directly to the role of the development professional. That is, the external environment must be continuously monitored for changes that may affect the well-being of the institution.

Contributions by Career Occupation. Doctors, lawyers, and directors of companies outperform the other occupations on all three measures of giving, while writers, academics, and educators consistently bring up the rear. It seems reasonable to assume here that career occupation is acting as an indirect and accurate measure of alumni giving capacity. Since law and medicine are the second and third most frequent career choices of Wesleyan alumni (Figure 3, Exhibit 3A), a clear fund-raising tactic with respect to career occupation emerges: A great deal of attention should be paid to alumni who are doctors and lawyers. As before, our findings do not point us in any new and surprising directions; this is the tactic already employed by development professionals at Wesleyan, just as it is at other institutions. Furthermore, it is not news that writers, academics, and educators do not contribute large amounts or in large numbers. However, there was one surprise in terms of how development professionals at Wesleyan *perceive* alumni generosity. Folklore has it that doctors and lawyers are very tight-fisted with their money, but our results indicate the opposite to be true. Although this new insight does not affect actual fund-raising strategy, it could very possibly influence the attitudes of fund raisers. That is, rather than thinking that soliciting contributions from these more affluent alumni is akin to pulling teeth, it may be that development professionals should have a more positive attitude. This might influence the bottom line: Any successful salesman will tell you that a positive attitude is the most important ingredient in getting the business.

Contributions by Geographic Region. Alumni loyalty appears to know no geographic boundaries for Wesleyan graduates living east of the Rocky Mountains. However, the participation rate for alumni living in the western United States is about five percentage points lower than in the other regions of the country (Figure 4, Exhibit 4B). Not unexpectedly, alumni living abroad contribute much less than their state-side counterparts (Figure 4, Exhibits 4B through 4D). Assuming that large gifts reflect both alumni loyalty and wealth, the pattern we observe in Figure 4 (Exhibit 4D) makes sense. Fewer alumni in the West make large contributions perhaps because it is difficult to maintain any sort of identity with the institution at such a great distance. Alumni in the East may give more because the converse is true, while alumni in the South may be older and more wealthy and thus able to make large contributions. The high median total giving for alumni in the South may follow from the same argument. Somewhat unexpectedly, Figure 4 (Exhibit 4C) shows that the median total gift of New England alumni is the lowest of the five regions. This finding may be explained if more younger alumni live in the New England states than in other regions of the country (that is, we know that younger alumni give less).

By going back to our data base, we can easily test these assumptions by taking a closer look at the demographics of alumni giving behavior. In doing so, we find that our assumptions are reasonable. Relatively more alumni living in New England are from the Classes of 1970 to 1980 than are alumni in the South (49.8 percent versus 41.7 percent, respectively). But unfortunately, it is not all that simple, because more young alumni from our sample live in the East (52.0 percent) than in any other region. Given these data and our argument, we would expect Eastern alumni to also contribute smaller amounts; instead, these alumni exhibit the highest rate of giving for amounts over $1000 and are second only to Southern alumni in median total giving.

To understand these facts, we have to go one step further by including career occupation in our demographic analysis. Could it be that the high proportion of young alumni living in the East is offset by alumni in this region holding jobs that are associated with higher levels of giving? This appears to be at least partly true; more alumni in the East are doctors, lawyers, and directors (the three most generous career categories) than are New England alumni (38.0 percent versus 32.1 percent, respectively). But again, it is not that simple. Relatively more alumni are doctors, lawyers, and directors in the Midwest than in any other region except the South, but graduates from the Midwest fall in the middle in terms of their generosity. Here we rely on the loyalty factor to explain this result by proposing that Eastern alumni may have closer ties with their alma mater than their Midwestern counterparts.

How do these findings inform fund-raising strategy? By combining the demographics of region and career occupation, we reach the inescapable conclusion that Wesleyan development professionals should concentrate their efforts on doctors, lawyers, and directors who live in the East. This advice is far from profound. Somewhat less obvious, however, is the recommendation that more effort might be well spent on Midwestern alumni, both with respect to soliciting large gifts and increasing the size of the median gift. A similar effort might produce positive results in the far West. In both cases, inroads might be made by devising ways to increase alumni loyalty, perhaps by regular newsletters or more frequent trips west by alumni affairs and development officers.

The most surprising result is that the median total giving of New England alumni is the lowest of the five regions. Our data suggest that this is not due to any lack of loyalty; the participation rate of New England alumni is the highest of all (Figure 4, Exhibit 4B). Rather, it seems to be related to more young alumni living in New England and fewer alumni pursuing high-paying careers there. In this case, attention should probably be paid to increasing the size of the median gift, especially as young alumni become better established in their careers. The pay-off from such an effort could be great, given the large number of Wesleyan alumni living in the New England area (Figure 4, Exhibit 4A).

Conclusions. All this has not told us anything that any development professional worth his or her salt does not already know: The giving behavior of alumni varies by class year, sex, career occupation, and geographic region in understandable ways. We maintain, however, that additional insight can be gained by stepping back and looking at these parameters in the aggregate rather than focusing on individual alumni. By organizing our variables with an eye toward microeconomic theory and fund-raising strategies and applying basic graphic techniques in their analysis, we have begun to develop a better understanding of fund raising as a dynamic process.

Measuring Alumni Motivation and Loyalty

The predictor variables we have been using so far can be viewed as indirect measures of the two alumni characteristics in Paton's functional model of giving: capacity and motivation. Our analysis suggests that career occupation holds promise for getting at alumni wealth and income, while class year seems to be a complex measure of both capacity and motivation (young graduates appear to hold more allegiance to the school, whereas older alumni are not as interested in the institution). Sex increases in importance as alumni grow older and geographic region has the least predictive power. As with class year, sex and geographic region are probably indirect measures of both motivation and capacity.

Although a thorough analysis of these measures has helped to increase our understanding of alumni giving behavior, the complexity of some of the paths prompted by our analysis suggests that our approach needs to be further developed. Along the same lines, Dunn (1985) has suggested that a more refined approach to modeling alumni giving behavior is needed to help in class-by-class planning, which lies at the heart of actual fund-raising operations. So where can we go from here? The model of alumni giving behavior suggests two complementary approaches: Develop better measures of (1) alumni capacity and (2) alumni motivation. The former has obvious appeal because it gets close to the bottom line, but has the drawback we mentioned above; people are usually not willing to provide this type of information. In addition, the institution cannot influence the income and wealth of its alumni, at least in the short term. In contrast, people are usually willing to express their opinion and attitudes about issues that are of interest to them. Take for example the numerous surveys on matter ranging from political campaigns to soda pop. Such data-gathering exercises are really attempts to measure the public's predisposition (a key ingredient of motivation) to vote for a particular candidate or use a certain product. With this information in hand, strategies are then devised to persuade the public to vote or buy in one's favor.

The motivational component of the functional model of alumni giving behavior thus holds the potential to be quantified and then influenced by taking advantage of the increased understanding provided by the gathering of new information. To accomplish these aims, the Development Office at Wesleyan has begun to survey Wesleyan graduates on a variety of issues, ranging from career-planning programs for students to supporting fund-raising goals of the institution. As described above, so far classes from years ending in 0 or 5 (that is, 1980, 1975, and so on) have been surveyed with a response rate averaging just under 50 percent. Of the over sixty items on the survey, we determined that twenty-two held promise as indirect measures of alumni motivation and loyalty. These items may be categorized as follows:

- support for student career planning activities (4 items)
- support for various fund-raising campaign goals (10 items)
- attitudes about ways to participate in a fund-raising campaign (4 items)
- knowledgeability of the Wesleyan Alumni Association (1 item)
- interest in the academic and cultural offerings of Wesleyan (1 item)
- attitude about class reunions (1 item)
- general question regarding support for Wesleyan's admissions, career planning, and fund-raising efforts (1 item).

Our questions are simple and straightforward. After the effects of class year, sex, career occupation, and geographic region have been accounted for, which (if any) of the survey responses help describe alumni giving behavior? By identifying the most important variables, can we gain a better understanding of alumni giving behavior? How might this increased understanding inform fund-raising strategies? Can any of the demographic and survey measures be used to help identify young alumni who should be contributing, or older alumni who should be making larger gifts? Although simple, these questions take us far beyond the methodology described above, emphasizing the need for a more refined approach.

A More Sophisticated Methodology. Discriminant analysis is the ideal technique to apply here. Simply stated, this procedure finds the combination of predictor variables that results in the best separation among the groups of interest and indicates whether or not the separation is significant. The linear combination of predictor variables is called the discriminant function and is very similar to the multiple regression equation with its associated regression coefficients. So far we have explicitly identified the predictor variables to be class year, sex, career occupation, and geographic region. The groups that we wish to separate, participants from nonparticipants, and large contributors from small contributors, have been implicitly defined by the y-axes of the graphs presented in Figures 1 through 4. In identifying the combinations of predictor variables in the function that contribute most to the separation of the groups, the analysis includes only the most important ones. Therefore, discriminant analysis is a simplifying procedure, for it holds the promise of going from many interacting predictor variables to a reduced set of measures that can be more easily understood (Kelly, 1982).

Coupling Analysis and Strategy. We direct our attention to class year by applying discriminant analysis to groups of alumni graduating in the same year. Presenting the results of the discriminant analysis for each of Wesleyan's surveyed classes, however, is clearly beyond the scope of this chapter. We choose instead to concentrate our efforts on the two classes that demonstrate most vividly the two major fund-raising strategies mentioned earlier. We speak here of the classes of 1970 and 1980, where we follow the second strategy with the former and the first strategy with the latter. The reasoning behind our choice of the class of 1980 is clear: They are young alumni. We think that the class of 1970 is appropriate in terms of the second strategy because these alumni are just entering their peak giving years (see Figure 1, Exhibits 1B through 1D), and hence have the greatest potential to make large contributions. We defined large contributions in the class of 1970 as total 1983-1985 giving equal to or greater than the third quartile, which was $300 (that is, the total contribution of one-fourth of these alumni was greater than $300).

We used the DISCRIMINANT procedure of SPSS (Statistical Package for the Social Sciences) and a DEC-20 computer to perform our analysis. This procedure provides a number of ways to enter and remove predictor variables. We chose to force all the demographic variables in first (sex for the class of 1980, career occupation, and geographic region), then enter the survey responses one by one until none met the criterion for entry. As variables are added, the program also checks if the discriminating ability of any of the variables already in the model has fallen to a point where it should be removed. We used the SPSS default criteria for entry and removal of variables (Norouis, 1985).

Dummy Variable Coding. Since sex, career occupation, and geographic region are qualitative (or discrete) measures, it is not possible to set up a natural scale to differentiate the various categories of each variable. For example, it makes no sense to code geographic region on a scale 1 to 6, where New England = 1, East = 2, West = 3, Midwest = 4, South = 5, and FA = 6. These are purely arbitrary assignments; any of the other possible coding schemes would have no more or less meaning. Since qualitative variables can influence the separation of groups like any other predictor variable in a discriminant analysis, the technique of dummy variable coding was developed by statisticians to handle these situations. In general, if a particular qualitative variable has r levels, we need to construct $r-1$ dummy variables. We do so by converting each variable to a set of dichotomous or two-level variables (lawyer versus non-lawyer, doctor versus non-doctor, and so on). The resulting sets of dichotomous variables can then be analyzed as if they were quantitative variables with defined scales of measurements (Dillon and Goldstein, 1984; Tabachnick and Fidell, 1983). We created three sets of dummy variables totaling fifteen in all: one for sex, nine for career occupation, and five for geographic region. The labels on Figures 3 and 4 indicate the actual categories; the student career occupation was used only for the Class of 1980. The "null case" (that is, all dummy variables equal zero) was "other" for career occupation and "FA" for geographic region.

Assessing the Importance of Predictor Variables. We assessed the relative importance of the predictor variables in separating the groups by examining the correlations between the discriminant function and the predictor variables in the model. SPSS accomplishes this by computing the value of the discriminant function for each alumnus and finding the Pearson correlation coefficients between the discriminant score and each of the original variables. The variables with the higher correlations are more closely associated with the discrimination. A table of the correlations between the discriminant function and predictor variables is commonly called a structure matrix, and can sometimes be useful in interpreting the function. Although consensus is lacking regarding how high a correlation for a predictor variable must be for it to be interpreted, correlations in excess of .30 are often considered eligible and lower ones are not (Tabachnick and Fidell, 1983).

Predicting Group Membership. Based on the coefficients of the discriminant function, the discriminant score for each alumnus can be calculated. These scores can then be used to classify (or predict) group membership of alumni (for example, those not contributing versus those making contributions). A perfect discriminant analysis would classify all alumni correctly, while one that produced no separation among the groups would perform no better than chance alone. Digging a bit deeper, it is possible that a statistically discriminant analysis performs well when it comes to classifying alumni who contribute, but not so well with noncontributors. On one side of the coin, this result might be telling us that we do not fully understand the behavior of noncontributing alumni and that we should search for additional measures that will increase the performance of our model. But looking at the other side of the coin, the misclassification of noncontributing alumni could also be an indication that these alumni should be participating in annual giving. While the first possibility has interesting theoretical value and may lead to increasing our understanding of alumni giving behavior, the second has immediate pragmatic value in that it may help identify noncontributing alumni who could be successfully solicited for gifts.

We used the "Confusion Matrix" option of the DISCRIMINANT procedure of the SPSS to obtain detailed information on the classification phase of the analysis. For each group, the number of correct and incorrect classifications, and the overall percentage of alumni classified correctly can be obtained (Norouis, 1985). The entries along the diagonal of the "Confusion Matrix" indicate correctly classified alumni since the predicted and actual groups are the same. Alumni in the cell above the diagonal are those graduates the model says should be contributing or making large gifts, but who are not. Entries in the cell below the diagonal are alumni who should not be participating or making large contributions. The latter result obviously has no pragmatic value in terms of direct fund-raising efforts. That is, we certainly do not want to go out and tell alumni not to participate or to make smaller donations because the model says they are not supposed to behave that way. Alternatively, as is the case with the alumni in the upper cell, these misclassifications are telling us that we do not fully understand giving behavior. By finding the additional measures that improve the classification rate, we may be able to fill in the missing pieces, which in turn should help to identify solicitable alumni.

Strategy 1: Get Young Alumni Involved

Of the 665 alumni in the class of 1980, 325 returned questionnaire forms for the 1985 Class Reunion Survey. However, we must offer the warning here that the composition of this sample is not representative of the class as a whole. Just over 50 percent of the Wesleyan's 1980 alumni participated in annual giving during 1983 to 1985, whereas over 75 percent of our survey sample made contributions. Therefore, noncontributing alumni are under-represented, which may limit the interpretations of the results and certainly the extent that the analysis can be used to identify nonparticipating alumni who should be making contributions. In addition, the DISCRIMINANT procedure dropped 152 alumni from the analysis because they had at least one missing predictor variable. During the classification phase, however, SPSS provides the option to classify cases with missing values by substituting them with means. We decided to take advantage of this option so that alumni who had only a few missing values would still be classified.

The discriminant analysis based on the 173 alumni from the Class of 1980 was statistically significant by anyone's standards ($p<.001$). That is, the linear combination of discriminating variables effectively separated contributing alumni from those who did not contribute during 1983 to 1985. The structure matrix (Table 1) shows that only five of the twenty-two survey items and two regional dummy variables were entered into the model. The dummy variables coded for technical careers, academic careers, and student all made it in. Examining the correlations in the structure matrix, we can narrow down the discriminating variables even further by applying the .30 criterion referred to above. In doing so, it becomes clear that only four variables are primarily responsible for separating the two groups of alumni. In short, the discriminant analysis has taken us from twenty-two survey items and fifteen demographic variables to a reduced set of four. We maintain that this represents a big step forward.

How can we interpret the four primary variables that appear in the structure matrix? Can this interpretation increase our understanding of alumni giving behavior? The first conspicuous characteristic of the structure matrix is that three out of the top four variables come from the survey; the dummy variable coded for technical occupations appears fourth on the list. The first two measures are clearly related to alumni motivation and loyalty, while the third item may represent a mix of both alumni capacity and motivation. All three variables are positively correlated with

Table 1. Structure Matrix for the Class of 1980

Variable	Correlation with Discriminant Function
Strengthen Admissions, Career Planning, and Fund-Raising Efforts	0.588
Expand and Modernize Library	0.469
Support Fund-Raising Goals	0.395
Technical Career	-0.326
Student	-0.200
South Geographic Region	0.147
Midwest Geographic Region	0.108
Make a Bequest	-0.104
Academic Career	-0.060
Make an Outright Gift > $25,000	0.041

the discriminant function, indicating that large function values (and hence alumni who contribute) are associated with positive responses to these items. Technical career occupations, however, are negatively correlated with giving behavior.

These findings strongly suggest that *within* the Class of 1980, traditional demographic measures are not very useful in describing alumni giving behavior. Rather, alumni attitudes about strengthening Wesleyan's admissions, career planning, and fund-raising efforts, coupled with support for expanding and modernizing the library, contribute most to producing the maximum separation between the two groups. In other words, participation in annual giving for these young alumni appears to be more a matter of loyalty than money (that is, the motivation factor of Paton's model seems to dominate over the capacity factor in determining whether young alumni choose to contribute). This would suggest that the development office should concentrate building on the existing loyalty of these young alumni without paying much attention to either demographics or their level of giving. This tactic goes hand-in-hand with the strategy that motivated the analysis: Get young alumni involved even if their average gift is small. Such efforts should have an immediate effect on the bottom line, for according to the discriminant model, the more alumni are involved with the institution, the more likely they are to participate in annual giving.

Predicting Alumni Giving Behavior. Almost three-fourths of the alumni were correctly classified (including those with missing values); if chance alone had been operating, less than two-thirds of the alumni would have fallen into the appropriate groups. However, the "Confusion Matrix"

(Table 2) indicates that the model experienced difficulty classifying noncontributing alumni, with almost half being placed in the contributing group. Who are these misclassified alumni? Perhaps there are yet unidentified measures that explain why these alumni are not contributing. They may in fact be alumni who should be contributing. In either case, the only way to find out is to contact each alumnus and ask him or her to make a contribution. If the response is negative, then the development professional might try to probe for the reason behind the reluctance, which will help increase our understanding of alumni giving behavior. If the response is positive, the bottom line will be increased.

A measure of the strength of each classification would also be a useful guidepost for the development professional. For example, it may be that the discriminant score of an alumnus clearly indicates that he or she should be included in one group or the other. The classification, however, may be equivocal if the discriminant score does not point clearly in one direction. With such knowledge in hand, development professionals would be able to anticipate how given alumni might respond to suggestions that they participate in annual giving, and thereby allocate development efforts accordingly. SPSS provides a measure that gauges the strength of classification by computing the probabilities of membership for each alumnus based on his or her discriminant score. The probabilities of group membership for the alumni misclassified in the contributing group are encouraging. Of these thirty-three alumni, over half (fifteen) of the twenty-seven alumni answering at least one of the three survey items heading the list of variables in the structure matrix were classified as contributors with greater than 75 percent certainty.

Strategy 2: Increase the Number of Large Gifts

The strategy of increasing the number of large gifts focuses our attention away from alumni who have not contributed in the last three

Table 2. "Confusion Matrix" for the Class of 1980

Actual Group	No. of Cases	Predicted Group Membership 1	2
Group 1 No Contribution	74	41 55.4%	33 44.6%
Group 2 Any Contribution	251	55 21.9%	196 78.1%

Percentage of alumni classified correctly = 72.9%

Percentage expected classified correctly by chance alone = 64.8%

years to those who have. We therefore define our sample here as all contributing alumni from the 394 members of the Class of 1970 who returned the 1985 Class Reunion Survey. Of these 153 alumni, 96 could be used in the analysis; however, as with the 1980 alumni, all were classified during the final phase of the analysis. About 30 percent of the sample made contributions during 1983 to 1985 totaling at least $300, approximating closely the 25 percent figure for the class as a whole.

The discriminant analysis was highly statistically significant ($p < .005$), and as before, it dramatically reduced the number of variables to consider. Of the twenty-two survey items, only five appear in the model, while only three demographic dummy variables were entered (two for career occupation and one for geographic region). Turning to the structure matrix (Table 3) we see that the survey items again dominate. However, the nature of the important variables is notably different from the Class of 1980. The first item listed in the structure matrix clearly touches on a money-related issue, while the second is the item we described above as possibly related to both alumni capacity and motivation. Both measures are positively associated with making large gifts. It is not until we get to the third variable in the structure matrix that we encounter an item clearly related to alumni motivation. The fourth measure might be considered a measure of alumni interest and has a negative correlation. The last interpretable entry in the structure matrix is the dummy variable for director or officer.

These results are telling us that the factors separating alumni who make large gifts from the rest of their classmates are dominated by survey measures, but are quite different than the factors that separate young alumni who contribute from those who do not. In the latter case, alumni involvement and motivation appear to be most important, while in the former alumni attitudes more closely related to capacity take precedence (that is, willingness to increase their annual gift and support fund-raising goals). There is even an indication that alumni interest in at least one aspect of the institution may be negatively associated with large gifts. In contrast, the positive association with plans to attend their class reunion suggests that older alumni who make large contributions may be more interested in their fellow alumni than they are in becoming involved directly with the institution. Finally, that being a director or officer of a company is associated with making large gifts parallels the finding described in the section on career occupations (see Figure 3, Exhibit 3D).

Taken together, these interpretations suggest that the development office should employ a different set of tactics to meet the strategic goal of increasing the number of large gifts than it does to secure the goal of the first strategy. Rather than encouraging alumni involvement in the institution, efforts should be made to keep alumni abreast of the activities of their fellow alumni, with an eye toward increasing alumni interest in reunion activities.

Table 3. Structure Matrix for the Class of 1970

Variable	Correlation with Discriminant Function
Substantial Increase WAF Gift	0.510
Support WAF Goals	0.488
Attend Class Reunion	0.382
Support Center for the Arts	-0.382
Director or Officer of Company	0.311
Law Career	0.271
East Geographic Region	-0.255
Support Student Financial Aid	-0.063

Encouraging alumni involvement in cultural activities, however, might not be a good idea. More attention should be paid to directors and attorneys than to alumni in the other career occupations. In short, the development office should let these older alumni know that the institution is sincerely interested in *their* activities. The results suggest that once this perception is established, there will be a better chance that alumni will express their interest in the institution by making larger contributions.

Predicting Alumni Giving Behavior. Overall, almost 75 percent of the alumni were classified correctly by the analysis; with chance alone operating, the expected rate of correct classifications is around 60 percent. The "Confusion Matrix" shows that the model performed quite well in classifying alumni whose contributions did not total $300 or more during 1983 to 1985 (Table 4). However, well over half of the alumni making large contributions were misclassified. In terms of increasing our understanding of alumni giving behavior, and hence perhaps increasing the bottom line in the long term, our next step should be to find out what additional information is needed to correctly identify alumni who are in fact making large contributions. With respect to increasing the bottom line in the short term, we should take a close look at the thirteen alumni who have been misclassified as large contributors; perhaps we will find that some of these older graduates are willing to increase the size of their gifts.

Upon examining these thirteen alumni, we find that they are not strongly classified as large contributors; the probability for membership in this group is over .75 for none of these alumni. However, a profile of these alumni constructed from the most important items in the structure matrix reveals that they fit nicely with the fund-raising tactics we suggested for the class of 1970. Specifically, ten of these alumni indicated that they were at least considering substantially increasing their annual gift, and eight responded positively to supporting fund-raising campaign goals. With respect to their

Table 4. "Confusion Matrix" for the Class of 1970

Actual Group	No. of Cases	Predicted Group Membership 1	2
Group 1 $0–$300	107	94 87.9%	13 12.1%
Group 2 >$300	46	28 60.9%	18 39.1%

Percentage of alumni classified correctly = 73.2%
Percentage expected classified correctly by chance alone = 57.9%

class reunion, seven were planning to attend. The career occupations of these alumni also fit nicely with our tactical suggestions: five are directors of companies and six are attorneys. Rounding out the profile, only five indicated they were interested in supporting fund-raising goals for the Center for the Arts. We feel that information like this could be of considerable value to the development professional in soliciting large donations.

A Final Comment

We wish to emphasize that we are making no claims for the development of new research methodologies. Rather, we have applied traditional graphic, survey research, and statistical techniques to help better describe and understand alumni giving behavior at a private liberal arts college. Our results indicate that we have taken the first step in the right direction. The real test will come, of course, when we attempt to apply what we have learned. That is, do the tactics suggested by our approach actually help meet the two major stategic goals of increasing the number of young alumni participating in annual giving and the number of large gifts from older alumni? We have confidence that they will, mainly because there is such a good fit between these tactics and fund-raising theory and strategy. We have tried to emphasize this point throughout the chapter. From a more fundamental perspective, we believe that our approach holds promise because it makes good sense, reflected by the fact that few surprises can be found in the results presented above. Rather, our findings serve more to reinforce in a systematic, quantitative, and predictive fashion things that development professionals have known about fund raising for quite some time. Thus, we in no way suggest that computer modeling can (or even should) take the place of what only the development professional can do best. Instead, we hope that our approach will help development professionals to better understand and predict alumni giving behavior, both on an aggregate and individual basis.

References

Dillon, W. R., and Goldstein, M. *Multivariate Analysis: Methods and Applications.* New York: Wiley, 1984.

Dunn, J. A. "Modeling Alumni/ae Annual Fund Participation: A Partial Success at a Liberal Arts College." Paper presented at the 12th annual conference of the North East Association for Institutional Research, Hartford, Conn., October 20-22, 1985.

Dunn, J. A., and Hutten, L. R. "Private Fund-Raising: A Comparative Study with Smaller and Larger Institutions." Paper presented at the 10th annual conference of the North East Association for Institutional Research, Hershey, Penn., October 16-18, 1983.

Kelly, K. S. "Pass the Alka-Seltzer: How Market Research Eases the Pain of 'Gut-Feeling' Solicitation." *CASE Currents,* 1982, *8* (5), 32-36.

McCaskey, C. G., and Dunn, J. A. "Look into My Crystal Cathode Ray Tube: Computer Models Make Giving Predictions Easy." *CASE Currents,* 1983, *9* (3), 38-42.

Norouis, M. J. *SPSSX Advanced Statistics Guide.* New York: McGraw-Hill, 1985.

Tabachnick, B. G., and Fidell, L. S. *Using Multivariate Statistics.* New York: Harper & Row, 1983.

Michael S. Connolly is institutional research consultant at Wesleyan University where he has been assessing the future direction and organization of institutional research. He also has consulted with faculty and administrators on a variety of projects, including the evaluation of the curriculum through an analysis of student course-taking behavior and the design of surveys to measure student attitudes.

Rene Blanchette is director of University Relations Research and Data Services at Wesleyan University. He designed the survey instrument to measure alumni attitudes described in this chapter. In addition to his fund-raising responsibilities, he consults closely with the University's Computing Center in the development of computer systems for alumni and prospect research.

To help the institutional researcher assess the institution's fund-raising activities and assist the development professional, a taxonomy of development planning considerations and of corresponding areas of collaboration are described.

Bringing It All Together

John A. Dunn, Jr.

The overall aim of this volume has been to stimulate interest among institutional researchers and planners in working with fund-raising and development personnel, for their mutual benefit and that of their colleges or universities. In this concluding chapter we bring together many of the notions presented earlier by putting ourselves in the position of the IR or planning professional who is asked to assess the performance of the institution's fund-raising activities and to assist in their advancement.

That task will be most constructive and informative if the researcher has a thorough understanding of the present and future plans of the development office. He or she can then contribute to the fact base on which the plan is built, and can evaluate at least some aspects of the plan itself. With the plan in mind, the analyst can also measure the effectiveness with which it is being carried out and the relationship between goals and achievements.

The assessment should begin with answers to simple but fundamental questions. These matters were addressed in Chapter One and Chapter Four but deserve restatement here. Is there a well-articulated plan that guides all dimensions of the fund-raising effort? Do these development objectives relate appropriately to the plans of the rest of the institution? And does the plan itself have an internally consistent and effective relationship between the *strategies* chosen by the president, governing board, and chief development officer, and the *tactics* and *tools* recommended by the development staff to achieve them?

In responding to these questions, the IR professional will have to rely more on common sense, organizational understanding, and logic than on quantitative analysis.

A standard recipe for successful fund-raising calls for three ingredients: attractive projects, prospects with the capacity and predisposition to give, and effective solicitors. While these are essential, we do not believe they alone are sufficient. We offer a broader taxonomy of factors in fund-raising planning, in the belief that, while not exhaustive, it will be provocative.

Strategic Questions

Strategic Fit. What is the overall strategy for the strengthening and enhancement of the institution, and where does fund-raising fit in? What is its relationship to other developments on campus, such as changes in the size or mix of educational, research, and service programs; recruiting strategies or needs; and facility and campus planning? Is the campaign to be used to help change an institution's image, internally or externally or both?

Goals. What are the specific objectives for which donations will be sought? What is the mix of endowment funds for faculty support, scholarships, or other purposes; facilities of various sorts; and operating support for ongoing or proposed programs? How attractive are these goals to prospective donors? What is the relationship of fund-raising goals from private sources to sponsored activity goals from public and private sources? Are the objectives balanced so that the institution will be able to support new facilities and programs on an ongoing basis?

Aspiration Level. How ambitious does the institution want to be? Where should its performance be relative to its peer group? What is its assessment of potential support? What resources can it assemble to pursue that support? Have the patterns of large and small gifts needed to reach the goals (giving tables) been carefully assessed?

Pacing. What is the length of time needed between major efforts—how frequently can the fund-raising accelerator be floored? Most institutions find periodic intensive fund-raising efforts (usually referred to as capital campaigns) useful not only in attaining specific objectives but also in raising ongoing fund raising to new levels. Nonetheless, this intensive effort needs to be interleaved with periods of fresh goal setting, revised planning, and new prospect research.

Timing. What is the relationship of fund raising, especially of major changes in style or goals or amounts, to significant events in the institution's history, such as new presidential leadership or important anniversaries?

Funding of Campaign Expenses. How will the institution cover the incremental costs, if any, of intensive fund-raising efforts? Remember that even if it only costs $0.14 to raise $1.00, a good investment in anyone's book, that still means that a $50,000,000 campaign is going to require spending $7,000,000.

Tactics

Audience. What is the mix of traditional and nontraditional constituencies that must be approached to achieve the goals? Note that the question is *not* what can known prospects give, but what constituencies will the institution have to *find* to reach the goal. What is the magnitude of the prospect research task? The answer will depend on the aspiration level, the goal mix, and the track record with each constituency. What is known about the prospects' capacity and predisposition to give? Can certain goals be assigned to specific constituencies? A special consideration here is the degree to which this decision implies working through existing alumni/ae organizations, or creating them, or going around them.

Depth vs. Breadth. To what extent will the dollars be sought by intensive cultivation of a small number of major prospects as opposed to broader solicitation? In part, answers here may depend on the strategic fit: For instance, if a campaign is part of an overall effort to change the image of the institution, broader solicitation may well be helpful even though it is relatively less cost effective than solicitation of major donors. Also, will the campaign have a quiet early focus on major donors whose gifts will give a reasonable assurance of achieving the overall goal, before proceeding to a more public phase?

Campaign Structure. Is an overall institutional campaign appropriate at this time, or should there be a series of more narrowly focused efforts? How is the fund-raising effort to be organized? Will everything be done from a central office or will there be school-based or regional programs as well? How will access to key prospects be managed? What will be the relationship of ongoing solicitation of annual support with the capital gifts effort?

Leadership and Solicitor Mix. What is the leadership responsibility (both in giving and in getting) of the board, the alumni organization, the deans, and the faculty? How should the work of asking be apportioned among board members, senior administrators, faculty, fund-raising staff, students (paid or volunteer), and volunteers? How effective are each of these solicitors? How are prospects assigned to solicitors?

Time Horizon. What length of time should the campaign run? This may depend on the decision on pacing.

Gift Types. What is the relative emphasis on deferred giving or on present cash and pledges? This answer may depend on the goal mix. Note, for instance, that scholarship and endowment goals seem to come mainly from bequests and other deferred gifts. To what extent should gifts other than cash and securities be sought—such as real estate, gifts-in-kind, joint ventures, operating businesses?

Piggy-Backing. Can particular goals be related to special events, such as school anniversaries?

Donor Relations. How should gifts and pledges be tracked and acknowledged, both on a current basis and in more permanent form?

Administration. How should fund-raising staff, other institutional personnel, and volunteers be motivated? How kept abreast of progress? How compensated or recognized?

Tools

Media Support. What are the publications and other materials, such as alumni magazines, fund-raising brochures, and related press coverage, that are directly or indirectly part of the fund-raising effort?

Solicitation Methods. Among the forms in which requests for support can be made, including written proposals, personal visits by individuals or teams, telephone requests, and mail appeals, what are the most effective for particular prospects and particular solicitors? You do not get if you do not ask; the trick is in finding the most cost-effective asker for each potential donor.

Events. What sorts of dinners, celebrations, reunions, press conferences, dedications, awards, and other such events can be used?

Activities. What are the best measures of each of the activities that compose a development effort, with respect to frequency, effectiveness, and cost? For prospect research, for example, one might use reports completed per researcher. For fund raisers on staff, one might use number of contacts, number of requests, amount requested, percent giving, and percent of requested dollars actually given.

With the taxonomy in place, it is easier to see how the institutional researcher or planner can help the development officer.

The researcher can properly be expected to evaluate *strategic decisions* only with respect to their internal consistency. These are policy matters for the chief development officer, the president, and the governing board. The researcher can, however, work with the development office in providing guidance to those making the strategic decisions:

- organizing and managing and analyzing surveys of potential donors for their attitudes about the institution and the attractiveness of particular goals
- analyzing where the institution is on the curve of marginal costs and marginal revenues
- comparing the institution's performance over time and with that of its peers, to help understand its own trajectory and competitive position
- analyzing recent giving patterns to judge the attractiveness and feasibility of various types of goals

- attempting an evaluation of the institution's overall potential for support, following Pickett's method (Chapter Four) or others
- projecting fund-raising progress and cash flow as part of the overall institutional plan.

Where the strategic decisions are clear, the institutional researcher or planner is in a good position to assess with the development office the *tactics* that have been chosen to achieve those ends and to contribute to their development:

- evaluating the tactics with respect to their fit with the strategic decisions
- surveying prospective donor constituencies for their knowledge and attitudes about the institution and its goals
- helping to identify prospect groups and individuals
- looking for patterns in the donations to the institution and to peer institutions in recent years that can help shape the tactics.

The third step is to look at the *tools* that have been chosen:

- evaluating the tools with respect to their fit with the strategic decisions and the tactics chosen
- assessing the effectiveness of publications in reaching their target audiences
- assessing the effectiveness of solicitors, activities, and events on whatever measures are selected.

Finally, the researcher or planner can play an important role in evaluating the results of the development effort with respect to the plans:

- developing and using methods for monitoring on a regular basis the gifts received and pledged, related expenditures, and cost-effectiveness
- conducting comparative studies of proceeds, progress, expenditures, and productivity with peer or aspiration groups
- assessing the institution's success in reaching its various constituencies
- analyzing actual and anticipated giving tables for the overall campaign and for each major component, to aid in subsequent planning
- measuring changes in perceptions and attitudes among those internal and external constituencies
- conducting analyses of the various fund-raising support activities in comparison to the plan.

To repeat: Our aim in this volume has been to stimulate interest among institutional researchers and planners in working with fund-raising and development personnel, for their mutual benefit and that of their colleges or universities. This book is an introduction; we look forward to many significant contributions to the field in the next few years!

Additional Reading

There is a paucity of material in the field, but the following are recommended:

Consortium on Financing Higher Education. *A Comparative Study of Development and College Relations at the COFHE Colleges.* Cambridge, Mass.: Consortium on Financing Higher Education, 1983.

Council for Advancement and Support of Education and the National Association of College and University Business Officers. *Gift Reporting Standards and Management Reports for Educational Institutions.* Washington, D.C.: Council for Advancement and Support of Education, 1981.

Dunn, J. A., Jr., and Adam, A. "Fund-Raising Costs and Staffing: A Comparison of Ten Private Universities, 1985." Paper presented at the NEAIR annual conference, Hartford, Connecticut, 1985a.

Dunn, J. A., Jr., and Adam, A. "Fund-Raising Proceeds: A Comparison of Twenty-Three Private Universities, 1976 to 1984." Paper presented at the NEAIR annual conference, Hartford, Connecticut, 1985b.

Dunn, J. A., Jr., and Hutten, L. R. "Private Fund-Raising: A Comparative Study with Smaller and Larger Institutions." Paper presented at the NEAIR annual conference, Hershey, Pennsylvania, 1983.

Dunn, J. A., Jr., and Hutten, L. R. "Finding the Ball-Park: Tufts Sets Fund-Raising Goals." *CASE Currents,* March 1984, pp. 30-34.

Dunn, J. A., Jr., and Hutten, L. R. "Private Fund-Raising Over Time: How Well Has It Kept Pace?" *Case Currents,* September 1985, pp. 44-46.

Dunn, J. A., Jr., Hutten, L. R., and Lotfi, S. "Private Fund-Raising Over Time: How Well Have Private Institutions Kept Pace?" Paper presented at the NEAIR annual conference, Albany, New York, 1984.

Dunn, J. A., Jr., and Terkla, D. G. "Private University Fund-Raising: Recent Achievements and Factors of Success." Paper presented at the AIR annual conference, Portland, Oregon, 1985.

Heemann, W. (ed.). *Analyzing the Cost Effectiveness of Fund Raising.* New Directions for Institutional Advancement, no. 1. San Francisco: Jossey-Bass, 1978.

Pickett, W. L. "What Determines Fund-Raising Effectiveness?" *CASE Currents,* January 1982, *8* (1).

John A. Dunn, Jr., is vice-president for planning in the Institutional Planning office at Tufts University.

Index

A

Achievement, measures of, 41
Adam, A., 3, 29, 38, 39, 53, 96
Administrators, and capital campaign, 14
Alumni: aggregate groups of, 70-71; analysis of giving by, 69-79; background on, 69-70; career occupations of, 73, 76-77; class year of, 72, 74-75; conclusion on, 88-89; demographics of, 71-79; discriminant analysis of, 80-83; geographic region of, 73, 77-78; graphics of, 70-79; large-gift strategy for, 86-88; measuring motivation and loyalty of, 79-83; participation rates by, 41-42; predicting giving by, 85-86, 87-88; reaching, 59; sex of, 72, 76; structure matrix of, 83-84, 86-87; survey of, 79-80; young, strategy for, 83-86

B

Bennett, R. L., 2-3, 7, 16
Beyer, K. G., 56, 67
Blakely, B. E., 56, 67
Blanchette, R., 3, 69, 89
Borton, G. L., 3, 55, 68
Broome, R., 1n
Buildings, fund raising for, 13

C

Cambridge Associates, 13, 16
Campaign effect, in capital campaign, 12
Capacity: and alumni giving, 69, 71, 74, 78; effects of, 22-23; predisposition combined with, 24-25; research on, 34-35
Capital campaign: analysis of, 7-16; background on, 7-8; feasibility of, 9-10; gift potential measures for, 10-12; objectives setting for, 8-9, 16; projections for, 12-13; resources for, 14-15; summary on, 15-16
Capital investment and consumption, issue of, 33-34
Carbone, R., 4
Career occupations, of alumni, 73, 76-77
Carnegie-Mellon University, economic impact of, 59
College and University Personnel Association, 49
Communications, and capital campaigns, 15
Comparisons: of achievement measures, 41; analysis of, 39-53; background on, 39-40; for capital campaigns, 15; of dependence on large gifts and trustees, 42; of environmental and organizational issues, 51-52; of expenditures, 44-49; normative, 37; of participation rates and gift sizes, 41-42; of proceeds, 40-43; of productivity, 49-51; of progress, 43-44, 45; simplifying assumptions in, 41; summary on 52-53; of trend analyses, 43
Connolly, M. S., 3, 69, 89
Consortium on Financing Higher Education (COFHE), 29, 30, 31, 32, 38, 96
Constituencies. *See* Donors
Corporations, reaching, 59, 64
Costs: average and marginal, 25-28, 32; concept of, 18; estimated, 30-32; interpreting, 32-36; measuring, 25-28; research on 29-32
Council for Advancement and Support of Education (CASE), 4, 5, 37, 43, 96
Council for Financial Aid to Education (CFAE), 1, 3, 29, 32, 38, 39, 40, 42, 60, 62, 65, 67
Council for the Advancement of Small Colleges (CASC), 29, 30, 31, 38

D

Demographics, of alumni, 71-79
Development, non-incremental alternatives in, 36
Development officers, and objective setting, 8-9
Development staff, and capital campaigns, 14
Dillon, W. R., 81, 89
Discriminant analysis: of alumni, 80-83; coupling analysis and strategy in, 81; dummy variable coding for, 81-82; and large-gift strategy, 86-88; predictions from 82-83; predictor variables for, 82; and young-alumni strategy, 83-86
Donors: alumni as, 69-79; capacity of, 22-23; controlling access to, 9; geographically distant, 64; identifying, 11; individual, 61-63; issues of, 93; new, 65-67; nontraditional, 60-64; predisposition of, 20-22; redirection of, 13; regionalization and travel for, 66; relations with, 94; researching, 56-58; traditional, 59-60. *See also* Private funding sources
Dunn, J. A., Jr., 3, 4, 5, 29, 31, 38, 39, 53, 71, 75, 79, 89, 91, 96
Duronio, M. A., 3, 55, 68

E

Economics of fund raising: and alumni giving, 69-89; analysis of, 17-38; application of, 32-36; background on, 17-18; and capital investment and consumption, 33-34; conceptual refinements in, 20-28; future of, 37; measuring costs and returns in, 25-28; predisposition and capacity in, 20-28; research in, 29-32; simple relationships in, 18-20
Edwards, R., 4
Effectiveness: measuring, 56-58; planning for, 58-59
Expenditures: by category of expense, 46; comparisons of, 44-49; giving related to, 18-20; progress versus, 49-51; by purpose, 46-49
Exxon Education Foundation, 4

F

Feasibility, of capital campaign, 9-10
Fidell, L. S., 81, 82, 89
Forman, R. G., 59, 67
Foundations, reaching, 59-64
Fund raising: activities for, 94; administration of, 94; and alumni giving, 69-89; amount of, 1; aspiration level of, 92; audience for, 93; campaign structure for, 93; with capital campaign, 7-16; comparisons of performance in, 39-53; depth vs. breadth in, 93; and donor relations, 94; evaluation for 94-95; events for, 94; expenditures in, 44-49; funding of, 92-93; gift types for, 93-94; goals of, 92; growth of, 55-56; institutional fit of, 92; isolation of, 2; leadership and solicitor mix for, 93; media support for, 94; microeconomic view of, 17-38; pacing of, 92; piggy-backing in, 94; from private sources, 55-68; proceeds of, 40-43; progress in, 43-44, 45; solicitation methods for, 94; strategy for, 92-93, 94-95; tactics for, 93-94, 95; taxonomy for, 91-95; time horizons for, 93; timing of, 92; tools for, 94-95

G

Gifts: from alumni, 69-79; average sizes of, 41-42; expenditures related to, 18-20; forms of, 65, 93-94; large, dependence on, 42; large, strategy for, 86-88; measuring potential, 10-12; potential for, 34; spendable, rate of receiving, 13; table of, for capital campaign, 11, 13; utility of revenues from, 35-36
Goldstein, M., 81, 89

H

Hall, M. R., 64, 67
Hays, J. C., 2-3, 7, 16
Heemann, W., 96
Higher Education General Information Survey (HEGIS), 40
Hutten, L. R., 71, 79, 96

I

Institutional research: on alumni giving, 69-89; and capital campaigns, 7-16; on comparisons, 39-53; fund-raising role of, 91-95; and microeconomics, 17-38; on private funding sources, 55-68

K

Kelly, K. S., 80, 89
Kotler, P., 56-57, 62, 67

L

Leslie, J. W., 29, 30, 31, 32, 34-35, 38
Lilly Endowment, 4
Ling, D. A., 4
Loessin, B. A., 3, 55, 68
Lotfi, S., 96
Loyalty. *See* Predisposition

M

McCaskey, C. C., 71, 89
McKenzie, P. C., 1*n*
Mail programs, for new donors, 65
Manos, S. S., 1*n*
Marketing and management information systems, for new donors, 65-66
Maryland at College Park, University of, research program at, 4
Massachusetts at Amherst, University of, data sharing at, 4
Mayer, N., 1*n*
Metropolitan Museum, 12
Microeconomics. *See* Economics of fund raising
Motivation. *See* Predisposition

N

National Association of College and University Business Officers (NACUBO), 4, 37, 43, 96
National Wildlife Federation, 12
Norouis, M. J., 81, 82, 89

O

Objectives, setting, 8-9, 16

P

Parents, reaching, 61-62
Participation, rates of, 41-42, 71-79
Paton, G. J., 3, 4, 17, 38, 53, 69, 71, 79
Peterson, M. W., 1*n*
Phone-othons, for new donors, 65
Pickett, W. L., 57, 67, 95, 96
Pittsburgh, University of: development office at, 3, 68; economic impact of, 59
Planning: issues in, 91; and microeconomics, 17-38; for private funding sources, 58-59
Pray, F. C., 66, 67
Predisposition: and alumni giving, 69, 71, 74-75, 76, 77-84; capacity combined with, 24-25; effects of, 20-22; measuring, 79-83; research on, 34-35
Private funding sources: analysis of, 55-68; background on, 55-56; conclusion on, 67; forms of giving from, 65; geographically distant, 64; individual, 61-63; intra-institutional alliances for, 63, 67; new donors as, 65-67; nontraditional, 60-64; planning for, 58-59; potential for, 57; regional friends as, 63; researching constituencies for 56-58; secondary affiliations as, 61-62; traditional constituencies for, 59-60; users as, 62-63. *See also* Donors
Proceeds, comparisons of, 40-43
Productivity, comparisons of, 49-51
Progress: comparisons of, 43-44, 45; expenditures versus, 49-51
Projections: for capital campaign, 12-13; concept of, 10
Prospects. *See* Donors

R

Ramsden, R. J., 29, 38
Reagan, R., 55
Returns: average and marginal, 28; concept of, 18; measuring, 25-28
Ridenour, J. F., 29, 31, 38
Rochester, University of, development planning at, 3, 38
Rowland, H. R., 56, 67

S

San Francisco Cable Car Foundation, 12
Smith, D. C., 56, 67
Stanford University, development professionals at, 2, 16
Statistical Package for the Social Sciences (SPSS), 81, 82, 83, 85
Support services, and capital campaigns, 14-15

T

Tabachnick, B. G., 81, 82, 89
Taft Corporation, 64
Terenzini, P. T., 1n
Terkla, D. G., 3, 39, 53, 96
Trustees, dependence on, 42
Tufts University, institutional planning at, 1n, 3, 53

V

Volunteers, and capital campaign, 14

W

Wesleyan University, development and institutional research at, 3, 70-89
Western Maryland College, research at, 29
Williams, W. K., 68
Willmer, W. K., 56, 66, 68